GROWING HERBS
A GUIDE TO MANAGEMENT

ROSEMARY TITTERINGTON

The Crowood Press

This book was conceived, designed and produced by The Oyster Press, Shaftesbury, Dorset.

First published in Great Britain in 1987 as *Growing Herbs* by
The Crowood Press
Gipsy Lane
Swindon
Wiltshire SN2 6DQ

Reissued in paperback 1990

British Library Cataloguing in Publication Data

Titterington, Rosemary
  Growing herbs
  1. Herb gardening
  I. Title
  635'.7 SB351.H5

ISBN 1 85223 555 1

Illustrations: Kimberley Bale
Design: Graham Beehag
Typesetting: Falcon Graphic Art Ltd, Wallington, Surrey
Printing and binding: Billings & Sons Ltd., Worcester

Contents

Dedication and Acknowledgements

I would like to dedicate this book to my grandmother, some of whose knowledge I absorbed unconsciously as a child, and my mother who has such faith in the beneficial use of herbs. My grateful thanks to my husband and family who were sure I could write a book, Ruth who patiently translated my writing and spurred me on, and Charmian Allwright who disciplined my ideas into a publishable form. I am pleased and proud to be known as a professional herb grower, but recognize how much I owe to people like John Hancock, Eric Bate, all my friends in ADAS and the herb and horticultural world from whom I have learned so much in the past years.

Latin names

The Latin names used throughout this book are those I have found to be the most commonly used by botanists, seed merchants, plant people and customers. As there is no absolute 'Bible' text to guide us on these names there will be plants that have more than one, or variations on the name which I have used.

Preface

Do you have a secret ambition to possess a beautiful and productive herb garden? Do you own some land which you feel could be producing an additional income? Perhaps you pause and daydream a little about the possibility of retreating to the country and growing herbs you love to use and cannot easily obtain in the shops. I have written this book for you!

It hardly matters whether you are just becoming aware of the delights of herbs, or that you have so many herbs in your garden that space is strictly limited. Once plants are flowing out of every spare pot, tub and old vase, it is clear that the fascination of growing herbs has entered your life and you will never cease learning something new and interesting.

There are many herb books, but very few give adequate information on how to actually start to grow herbs for pleasure and profit. The enormous problem is how to enjoy being a herb grower and to make some money at the same time! I have not yet met a rich herb grower, but it is possible to make a reasonable living and enjoy doing it.

This book is mainly practical common sense and the result of many years' experience. Some simple commercial and professional principles will assist those who wish to grow sufficient herbs to supply home, friends and relatives. It will also help to smooth the way for many who would like to expand an enjoyable hobby into a thriving business.

Rosemary Titterington, 1987
Iden Croft Herb Farm, Kent

I
What shall I do?
How shall I begin?

The first question to ask yourself is what type of herbs would you like to grow, and if you wish to obtain some financial return from your efforts – who will buy them? If you are one of the fortunate few who have immediate customers ready and waiting on your doorstep, then the decision has probably already been made. For most of us though, the initial and most important step is to first find and thoroughly research your market! You may, in your opionion, have produced the most wonderful plants, but if there is no one to buy them they will languish unsold and cost you good money. Demand may be created, but surviving at the same time may prove difficult and disappointing unless you have other sources of income.

Fortunately herbs and their uses are well publicized in advertisements, magazine articles, food programmes on television and in books. Herb products may be seen everywhere promoting the image of health, beauty, flavour and natural living. At least you are thinking of producing plants or products that are becoming increasingly popular. The problem lies in selecting what type of herbs to grow after your careful research, and then gaining the requisite experience to fulfil the demand. The main areas to research as a prospective herb grower are dealt with in this chapter.

Herb Plants

Retail Nursery

An obvious, interesting choice for anyone with a reasonably sized gardening population nearby.

Wholesale Nursery

If the nursery is isolated or has problems with access (eg rights of way or no parking), the production of plants for selling to other nurseries, shops and garden centres could be a wise choice. There is a rising market for supplying small plants to growers whose propagation areas have become too small for their requirements. Plant production for wholesale and retail supply can be done successfully if the facilities and labour are adequate and transport for delivery is available.

Mail order plants

Not a wise choice at first, in my opinion. You are remote from the customer and it requires a wide range of plants or unusual herbs of special interest to persuade someone to actually pick up a pen and place an order. Special offers of plants are always an unknown quantity and produce a variable response, anything from 500 to 12,000 orders!

Large plants

These are used by garden designers, landscape architects and for amenity planting. It takes time to produce large, quality plants and is a good idea to always have a few for displaying at shows etc. Liaise with a garden design firm about their future requirements, and grow them attractive plants. Enhance their reputation – and your own!

Fresh-cut Culinary Herbs

Retail

Cut herbs can be sold direct to the public from the nursery, either to be collected, or delivered to them on a regular basis. This is not usually a large trade, and can be very time consuming if not properly organized. To run up and down the nursery paths for a small order of Chives can make the actual bunch of herbs quite expensive from your point of view!

Direct to local establishments

These can include hotels, restaurants, health food stores, farm shops, and greengrocers. This form of marketing takes time to promote, and requires some form of food packaging plus a regular delivery service. You will need a knowledge of catering requirements, seasonal foods and even the dates of all religious festivals can be helpful. Herbs are used in many delicious ethnic dishes but are not going to be required at times when fasting is taking place (ie during Ramadan), or if a traditional dish using only certain herbs is prepared for Feast Days.

The continuity of supply is very important; nothing irritates a customer more than an erratic service. If the menu has been printed and Dill is not available for the salmon, or Coriander for the curry, the chef will conclude that you are unreliable and look for an alternative supplier.

Supermarkets

These are usually supplied through central purchasing and distribution divisions. All kinds of food regulations have to be observed, which involves using equipment that can be quite expensive. The art lies in stimulating public demand so that herb packs are picked up and examined and then placed in the trolley, not put back on the shelf!

Wholesale markets

It is worth while researching the local wholesale market; these are usually very busy, being used by shops and small res- taurants in the area. The main London markets have been supplied regularly for years, but local markets may be unable to obtain supplies on such a basis. It is a gambler's market and fluctuates throughout the year; a run of bad weather can affect buyers. Weather affects everyone's mood. In rain, people go to restaurants less frequently, and menus change, becoming unseasonal. As the sun breaks through, a sense of buoyancy and optimism pervades the market and sales will alter again –

human nature plays an unexpected role. The average prices over the year can be good if herbs are scarce in your area. It is most important to have a good regular supply available so customers know where they can always find your herbs.

Food-processing industry

These companies usually require bulk supplies grown to their own particular standards and requirements. It is an expanding market, but there is the chance that a particular product may be suddenly eliminated. This situation could leave you with a large unsold crop.

Fresh Medicinal Herbs

The growth of public interest in alternative medicine has created a small demand for fresh medicinal herbs. It is worthwhile investigating local alternative health clinics and individual practitioners in case they have difficulty in obtaining a particular herb. A higher price may be expected, but organic growing would probably be essential, and clear instructions should be obtained for harvesting at the correct stage of growth.

Dried Herbs

Experience in growing and drying herbs on a small scale is invaluable if you would like to expand into a large venture in the future. There may be some herbs – eg Marigold flowers – that are a better colour if dried in small quantities.

Culinary

Many herb growers produce beautiful dried herbs as a side-line to another herb enterprise. Quite large areas of herbs need to be grown in order to make a viable income. If you are likely to be encouraging tourists, an attractive pack of locally grown and dried herbs can be a popular purchase.

Medicinal

Imported herbs are so low in price that quality, accuracy, and usually quantity are essential considerations to ensure that your own herb crop produces sufficient return on investment. Liaison with a local health clinic or practitioner would be worthwhile.

Aromatic Herbs

Some herbs with aromatic leaves and/or flowers are a pleasure to grow, dry and blend. Good presentation is advisable if they are to be packaged, and they should be stored in a dry place. Bunches of dried flowers and leaves for decorative use are very popular in the autumn and early winter when flowers are in short supply.

Show and Demonstration Gardens

These projects can be time-consuming unless carefully planned. They are a good way of promoting sales of plants and herb products, and useful when running courses and lectures.

Frozen and Freeze-dried Herbs

These are used mainly in the production of large quantities of prepared food, stuffings, sauces etc. This is not an easy market unless you are prepared to 'think big' or become a contract grower. The home freezing of certain herbs for domestic use can be very successful, but specialized machinery is required to prepare frozen herbs to the standard required for the food industry. Freeze-dried herbs are mainly imported at present.

That is only a brief outline of the main uses and markets for herbs. There are many more to be explored – it is up to you!

2

Setting up ~what is involved?

If you were thinking of buying a house, you would probably start by having a large number of requirements in advance, then finally choosing the one which fulfilled most of your ideals.

The perfect herb garden, nursery or herb farm would be well drained, sheltered from prevailing winds and with a southern aspect (shade can always be created). The soil would be easily worked, not too rich, and mid-way between acid and alkaline. Water would be plentiful and easily available at a good pressure from the mains or reservoir. Customers of the kind you prefer would be on or near your doorstep and spare land would be available (at a low rent!) should you wish to expand. If greenhouses and other buildings are already there, they would be well sited and in good repair. Permanent sound paths and driveways of sensible widths – excellent! A well-constructed boundary of rabbit fencing, a beautiful view to look at when you straighten up. A dream cottage discreetly hidden in a plants-man's garden. Add to all this any personal requirements such as good schools, adequate train services, ideal distance from relatives etc., and you will soon realize that the perfect place does not exist.

We can all dream, but most herb growers find reality falls far short of the foregoing description and yet they succeed by adapting what is already available. My own experience is that I fell in love with the soil and the situation, ignored the dilapidated greenhouses and general muddle, and had to forget all about the dream house!

Heavy waterlogged land facing north, difficult access, badly sited buildings are all difficult problems to overcome and should not be ignored if you do not want to spend years slaving away fruitlessly for success.

Soil

This is the basis of plant life and should be respected. I really resent hearing it called 'dirt'! I feel it should be kept 'alive' with humus, carefully planned cultivation and earthworms.

Simple observation of the soil on your prospective herb-growing area, by means of hand and eye, can tell you quite a few important things. Is the soil hard and dry with deep cracks, waterlogged after rain, sticks to your boots, forms into a greasy ball when held in the hand? Think carefully, it may be heavy clay: cold and wet in winter, baked hard in summer, difficult to work at the appropriate time for seed-sowing and planting, heart- and back-breaking. However, console yourself if you already have it – clay can be very fertile when drained and after plenty of bulky humus and coarse material have been worked into it. Just don't attempt to deal with too large an area at one time if suitable machinery is not available.

If the soil is very light and sandy, it can be marvellously easy to work at most times of the year. It will warm up early in the spring and excess water will drain away rapidly in winter. It will also suffer from drought while plant nutrients will be washed out rapidly in a wet season!

Most soils will vary between these two extremes, the 'ideal' soil being a balanced mixture of sand, silt and clay. To ascertain the type of soil take a spade and dig a hole to see what the subsoil looks like; inspect for earthworms – a sign of good soil health. A good soil should be of a fairly uniform colour down to a foot or 15″ after which it will merge with the subsoil. If it has greyish or brownish flecks these could indicate a need for drainage and advice should be obtained. Look at plant roots to see if they are large and go deep down (another good sign) or are they stunted and matted sideways, indicating a high water table, poor drainage, or chemical residues. If you strike a hard layer, it may be rocky subsoil, hard clay or even Roman remains. The most likely reason for this condition on cultivated land is compaction of the soil into a layer which is impenetrable, caused by using machinery or walking on it when it is wet. The solution is to 'shatter the pan' (or hard layer) by means of a chisel or mole drainage plough, a pickaxe (if working a small area), or even by old-fashioned double digging.

Look at the Weeds

How many perennial weeds can you see? Creeping Thistle, Couch grass, Docks, Ground Elder, creeping Buttercup and Oxalis are devils to eradicate. They can be cleared by chemic-

CREEPING BUTTERCUP

BROAD DOCK

COMMON COUCH

als, but you will never be awarded an organic symbol! It takes time to fallow land and treat it overall, although a green manure of rapid crops, such as Mustard, annual Lupins or Rye grass, grown for a season will improve fertility. Later, spot treatments with hormone weedkillers are effective, but one will always have to be on the offensive against recurrence.

Soil types are betrayed by the plants that grow on them. Lush Nettles, Chickweed and large 'soft' weeds may indicate rich, fertile (and damp) land. Poor, pale growth could show low fertility and low soil health, or lack of moisture. If there is no weed growth at all, and the land appears bare and clean, you need to know what chemicals have been used recently, and are there any chemical residues that may affect sensitive plants in the future? Moss, Dock and Sorrel favour an acid soil. Coltsfoot is common on poor gravels, while impeded drainage produces Rushes and Buttercup. Look out for these plants they are a valuable source of information about your land.

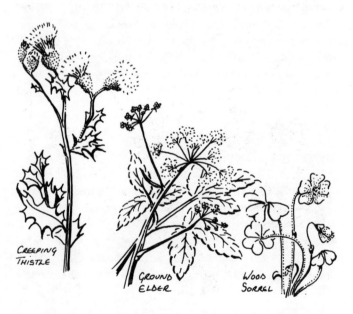

CREEPING THISTLE

GROUND ELDER

WOOD SORREL

Aspect

It does help enormously to have a warm, wind-sheltered site, unless you live in a part of the world where the sun shines all day long, and shade is essential to prevent the plants from scorching. Wind is a far greater enemy to plants than most people realize.

The ideal windbreak filters about fifty per cent of the air, and prevents turbulence forming on the leeward side. Many different windbreak materials are available these days and are illustrated in the various trade and gardening magazines. They can be of the knitted or nylon mesh type or of an almost rigid plastic with different-sized holes; the plastic kind should last for up to ten years. Of course, the value of trees and hedges should be remembered if space is not limited.

Do make sure that the fence supports are stronger than at first appears necessary, with good straining posts at the corners. We dread high winds, which are nearly always at their worst in the middle of the night. It's not much fun at this hour, in the rain and darkness, trying to disentangle and save a length of nylon before it disappears into a neighbour's orchard.

It is interesting how many horticulturalists become compulsive weather forecast fans. I often wonder how many growers are 'doing the rounds' on a late-night check after a sudden frost or gale warning.

Layout and Access

The layout of a nursery or garden is usually well established for good or ill when purchased. It can be almost more bewildering when you are faced with a blank expanse and only have a muddled picture of what you actually want to do.

Try to get your objective clear in your mind, and list what you feel you will need. Then enlarge it all a little – the tendency is to have too narrow a path, too small a potting area, too few herbs! Remember about motion and time. Try to plan logically the shortest distances between potting and standing grounds for pots, with collecting or packing sheds near to the transport-loading area, and even plan where to have an electric plug for making the coffee or tea to restore you, when it seems a waste of time to return to the kitchen.

Vehicles collecting and delivering seem to get larger year by year, and the drivers can become quite short-tempered if it is difficult to manoeuvre and turn around. If you don't want to wheel all the compost on a small barrow from the roadside, make sure that your access is wide enough to take quite a large lorry. I must confess I speak from experience – if just a few badly parked cars are preventing easy turning, an articulated lorry or very large coach can cause havoc on our herb farm.

Frequently used paths should be of concrete, paving or gravel – something that will stand up to constant use in all weathers, and wide enough to take wheelbarrows, trolleys or two people passing each other. Less-used paths of hard-wearing grass need mowing, but do look attractive and provide a framework for the plants.

In later chapters you will find the requirements for different types of herb growing, and from these you should be able to plan and adapt your own land.

Frost and Wind Protection

To extend the season early in spring and late in autumn, some kind of protection is usually required. The simplest and cheapest form for rows of plants is low polythene tunnels over wire hoops.

If you have glass cloches (usually stored in old nurseries), they can be very useful in the early stages of setting up, but time-consuming in the long run. If cropping under glass cloches, a useful tip is to remove and set aside the first cloche, and then move each one down a place as one works along the row. Finally replace the first cloche in the last space worked.

Simple cold frames can be created by using railway sleepers and covering them across with polythene, held down by wooden battens. There is an enormous variety of polythene and polycarbonate covers now available, so that one can buy what can be afforded at the particular time.

The prices of large polythene tunnels are still very reasonable and these are excellent for covering land to withstand the worst of the winter. They vary in length and width and are fairly easy to erect. Having said that, I would not advise you to start erecting a very large one without help, or experience. In practice we have found the smallest useful size to be 14 ft (4·2m) in width by 60 ft (18·2m) long. Firms who specialize in the manufacture of polythene tunnels are usually most helpful with advice and instructions – some will also build the tunnel for you, or provide a list of firms who offer such a service.

If you can run to the extra expense, open-mesh plastic along the base at the sides of the tunnel will allow plenty of air

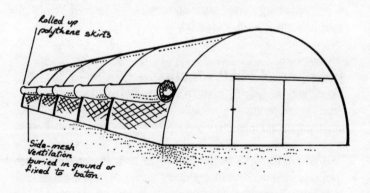

through for ventilation. The plastic cover itself can be rolled up during warm weather and rolled down again as required. The heat build-up in a polythene tunnel in a hot summer has to be experienced to be believed.

Glasshouses are wonderful buildings to own and use, if they are not of ill-fitting, old glass, with rotten benches, inadequate heating, high unsafe ridges and harbouring all the nastiest pests and fungi possible. However, even in this condition they *can* be of use; a new greenhouse, of sufficient size for propagation and winter storage of half-hardy plants, can be very expensive.

If you do have an old greenhouse, take heart and really clear out the rubbish and generally clean up. Use a suitable disinfectant (I'm a Jeyes' Fluid or formaldehyde fan), according to the manufacturer's instructions, and thoroughly wash and repair the glass using modern sealing tapes.

An old greenhouse can add an air of stability and continuity to a nursery and can be made to really work for you. If it is well lined in winter with one of the modern anti-condensation lining films, and heated by a simple automatic, natural or bottled gas 'hotbox' heater, you will find that it is not only a good workplace, but a comfortable retreat in cold weather. There is always something to be done there!

A shade house can be a great asset, not only in summer for shade-loving plants, but in winter to provide wind protection for those plants which will not suffer from low light levels. Shading is available in various materials and durability. The most important point to consider is the percentage of light allowed through to the plants. Thirty per cent shade really does mean that seventy per cent of the light available will reach the plant, and that will be cut down by the additional shade cast by the construction necessary to hold the shade material in place. There may be naturally shady and cool places in the garden or nursery, which can be utilized during the summer – but not if they are too far away from the main area of activity.

Out of sight, out of mind, and do not forget that slugs, snails and rampant weeds love shady places too!

Space Heating

This can be simple and basic, just sufficient to protect against frost for half-hardy plants, and to start into early production. I have found that an old-fashioned double oil burner will cope with an area up to 600 sq.ft (55 sq.m), except in the most severe weather in the south-east of England. For greater peace of mind, and to maintain higher temperatures an automatic, natural or bottled gas 'hotbox' heater is excellent and simple to install. Electricity, solid fuel and oil all have their advantages and problems – usually cost! Large areas and more precise heating requirements should be discussed with an expert, bearing in mind your particular situation.

The Electricity Board has a horticultural advisory section, which provides excellent leaflets on the use of electricity, cable installation and space heaters, so do consult them about the safe use of electricity. It is always wise to have a professional electrician check your wiring and plugs for safety if you have done all the work yourself.

Much can be done to conserve the natural heat of the day by lining polytunnels and greenhouses with insulating material. There are several types from which to choose, from thin plastic film which will trap a layer of air, to bubble film which is available in different sizes. If you look around your local garden centre's sales greenhouses you will probably see several types in use and be able to assess which would be most practical for you. A staple gun will fix the material firmly in place on a wooden frame, while metal-framed houses have specially designed clips with which to attach the insulation. In polytunnels a thin film of the material can be drawn over the hoops beneath the cover and left slack enough to form an insulating space. Make certain that all windows and doors fit tightly without warping, and fit plastic 'draught excluders' across the entrance of each tunnel inside the door frames.

Propagation Systems

The reason for having a propagating bed is to speed the rooting of cuttings and encourage the germination of seedlings as quickly as possible, so that they may grow away sturdily without check through wilting or disease. The idea is quite simply to provide heat at the base of the rooting medium and sufficient humidity around the cutting to keep it from wilting and dying before it can begin forming roots. There are many ways of doing this, from cheap simple but time-consuming methods to expensive layouts which you can leave happily for days.

I have progressed from a simple box frame with a polythene cover placed over soil-warming cables in a greenhouse bed, to a heated sand bed and mist unit, and also heated sheets. I feel that the experience and knowledge gained in the early stages

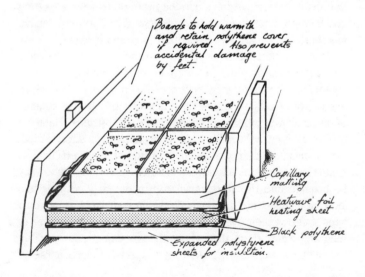

Boards to hold warmth and retain polythene cover if required. Also prevents accidental damage by feet.

Capillary matting

'Heatwave' foil heating sheet

Black polythene

Expanded polystyrene sheets for insulation.

through observation and frequent checking of the cuttings has helped me to know just what I am doing with a larger more automatic unit. We still use all the various methods, so don't be despondent and feel unprofessional if you have to start with a simple DIY system. If it is possible to construct a bench sandbed containing soil-warming cables in a greenhouse, a single row of hoops and perforated polythene cover placed over it can be most effective in maintaining humidity.

A new type of heated foil sheet is available in different lengths to provide base heat for propagation, and it has the added advantage of being removable if you have sited it in the wrong place. Insulate it from the ground with polystyrene sheets, and use capillary matting on the top. Advertisements for these sheets can be seen in trade magazines, and the address of the principal manufacturer may be found on page 156.

Stock and Stock Beds

This is a very important part of the garden or nursery, and one that is frequently overlooked in the first enthusiasm of 'setting up'. For good propagation and healthy plants you must have stock plants that are large, healthy, pest and disease free, as well as being true to their variety. Set aside an area specially for stock plants, either planted in the ground or in large containers. If using the latter these should be large enough to encourage healthy root growth. It is sensible to have a number of herbs growing for the production of early cuttings. Having a healthy root growth enables a plant to support good top growth which will afford plenty of healthy cuttings and also enable it to renew itself fairly rapidly. Stock plants in large containers may be brought into the glasshouse to provide early cuttings and later be plunged into beds outside. Have your stock plants on a special site of their own, with clear labelling, and remember to feed and water them throughout the season.

Do buy your initial stock from a specialist herb nursery,

which should be able to supply accurately named plants. (See page 155). To protect the public there are British Standards for the thirty most popular culinary herbs – so make sure you are familiar with them. The information is available from the British Standards Sales Dept. (See *Other useful publications*, page 154 for complete details.)

The British Herb Trade Association holds meetings regularly for herb growers, and these gatherings are invaluable for new members in expanding their knowledge and recognition of plants.

Tools and Equipment

If asked, most growers would immediately name their favourite tools, and then think hard about the uses of the rest of the collection in their tool shed. Most good tools feel comfortable, like an extension of hand and muscle to ease and

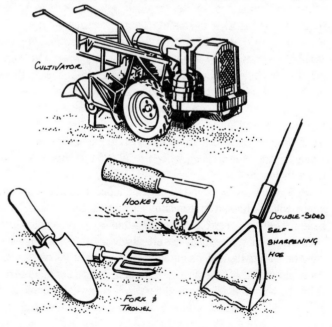

speed a particular job. On my personal list would be a stainless-steel small trowel and fork, of the right weight and size for me. My favourite is a 'hookey' tool, shaped like a flat claw, which is marvellous for cleaning cracks, pavings and tidying up show beds. I use a small border fork and spade, as I have the theory that I am always tempted to lift too much at a time, and a strained back would prevent me from lifting anything at all. The flat, two-sided, self-sharpening hoe is the fastest one I know, and is also the best for use with a straight back. We have many more varieties of hand tool for various purposes; some very old-fashioned ones and others, I regret to say, pristine from little use, having not fulfilled their promise. I feel it is essential to suit the tool to the job. Small areas of weeds can be cleared with the aid of a jumbo-sized nylon ground-sheet and wheelbarrow (with pneumatic tyre), larger areas using tractor and bin or trailer.

For cultivating the soil and preparing seed beds in larger areas, a cultivator is essential. There are many types and sizes, and working demonstrations of their various abilities can usually be arranged by firms specializing in garden and horticultural machinery. County shows generally have quite a number on display, and other growers will usually talk at length about good and bad points of the particular make which they have in practical daily use. Do try and see the machines in action on the toughest job you will wish to undertake. Cultivating an already well worked piece of soil will not show whether it can tackle real work.

Small tractors have now become commonplace, not as estate toys but used in conjunction with all the scaled-down implements you might require on a nursery, or small farm. They are small enough to operate inside an 18 ft (5.5m) wide single-span polytunnel, and powerful enough to tackle the chisel-ploughing of a small field. Do insist on four-wheel drive and front weights, whatever the salesman says! We looked at all the makes available before we finally bought a new tractor.

The deciding factor was the continuing advice and after-sales service offered by one particular firm. They were able to analyse all our requirements, advise on and, if necessary, adapt tools for our own specialist needs.

Climate

If I decided to grow herbs in another part of England, or indeed anywhere in the world, one of my first areas of research would be to find out exactly what was grown already in my chosen neighbourhood, looking first in gardens, then fields and then commercially. The local gardening club or horticultural association can be a mine of information as they tend to know all the local problems and the vagaries of the climate, as well as being prepared to talk about them. Time spent in research *can* save some expensive mistakes. The ADAS can provide local information on both soils and climate. In each region there is an Agro-met Adviser, who can give you likely rainfall, temperature ranges and frost frequency of any site (see p.151).

What Will All This Cost?

This is extremely difficult to estimate. Many people start with very little capital and are most successful, but it takes time and determination. Others start with more money and then find they have invested capital in equipment no longer in use, because their growing methods or outlets have changed.

The only answer is to gather all the catalogues, lists, trade papers, quotations together, and list all your possible requirements. Go down the list again, being totally honest, and underline the items that you cannot do without. Price and keep for future reference all the items you would love to use and have, but which are not strictly necessary – perhaps they can be bought from your first few years' profit!

It is illuminating how one's priorities change when actually running the business; but whatever you do it is a good idea to keep some funds for emergencies.

3
Growing herb plants in pots

How many plants for the house and garden did you buy during the past year? I'm sure you were tempted in spring to rush out and look round a nursery or garden centre to buy 'something' to fill in a blank space after the winter losses. The idea of herb pot plant growing is attractive to anyone with 'green fingers' and a love of gardening. One of the many advantages is that your stock is visible, and need not be at the mercy of the weather. It is also rewarding to be able to satisfy the spring and summer demand caused by the English passion for gardening. Even when traces of snow remain, the first weak sunshine of spring brings out the keen gardeners from their winter slumber! Here lies the problem – they arrive expecting to find plants full of foliage and vigour to replace their old favourites that have died during the winter. Gardeners are eternal optimists, and this points up the main difference between growing for a hobby and selling to the public.

In commercial practice you are always growing 'out of season' to produce plants for sale to meet the early demand when the public are most enthusiastic about buying! This involves skilful planning of growing seasons, propagation and seed sowing, and the provision of adequate protection against late winter frosts and damaging wind. Even hardy plants can become somewhat bedraggled if just left to the ravages of the average English winter.

A common question put to me by newcomers to the nursery trade is 'How many plants shall I require?' I always feel tempted to give the short answer 'Enough!' In pot plant production you have to take into account type of outlet, size of your propagation area, amount of standing-out room available; only *you* can do the necessary calculations so that you can assess what is a manageable amount. This quantity will also be limited by the time and labour available.

Propagation

I recommend the comprehensive book by Alan Toogood called *Propagation*. Other excellent advice and plant lists are to be found in books listed in the Appendix (see pages 153-4).

To refresh your memory about plant categories, annuals are plants which produce leaf, flower and fruit and then die at the end of the season. Biennials grow over two seasons, usually flowering in the second. Perennials grow over many seasons, increasing in size and thus requiring division when they grow too large.

It is a good idea to follow the basic methods for propagation. When you are familiar with the habits and characteristics of particular plants, you can then experiment with confidence at any time of the year knowing what you are trying to achieve. These methods are essential for all herb growing because propagation is mainly done by means of cuttings and the division of mature plants.

Herbs are fairly easy plants to propagate – from seed, from cuttings and by root division. Almost all herbs can be raised from seed but as not all seed will be accurate, true varieties of plants should be stocked bearing the correct names. Plants which are a hybrid (i.e. the result of crossing two species) will not grow true from seed, being sometimes variable and showing differences in colour, form and size. Vegetative propagation is necessary with most types. There are British Standards on the accuracy and quality of thirty of the most popular culinary herbs sold in Britain; it is therefore sensible to obtain a copy of these from the British Standards Institution (address on page 151).

Seed sowing

Herbs usually raised from seed include Alexanders, Alkanet, Angelica, Anise, Basil (annual), Borage, Burdock, Caraway, Celery leaf, Chervil, Chives, Chamomile (German), Coriander, Cumin, Dill, Fennel, Foxglove, Heartsease, Holy Thistle, Jacob's Ladder, Lady's Mantle, Lovage, Marigold, Marjoram (sweet), Melilot, Milk Thistle, Mullein, Nasturtium, Orach, Parsley, Purslane, Rocket, Safflower, Salad Burnet, Savory (Summer), Sage (annual Clary), Sorrel, Sweet Cicely, Vervain, Woodruff (annual).

Requirements

1. Seed from a good commercial source.
2. Compost, a proprietary seed compost;
   or 70% fine peat, 30% sharp sand, well mixed;
   or 50% fine peat, 50% fine forest bark.
3. Clean seed trays or pots.
4. Board for firming compost.
5. Labels and pen for noting variety and date.
6. Fine sieve.

Method Fill all the requisite number of trays or pots in advance, level the surfaces and gently firm with a board. Water with copper fungicide (Bordeaux Mixture) to prevent 'damping off' (plants wilt at the seedling stage) and allow to drain until nicely damp, not wet. Sow the seed thinly and sieve more compost gently over the seeds to just cover. The general rule is to cover with a depth of compost equivalent to the size of the seed. Label with name and date and place the containers on a warm bed, covering with glass, plastic or newspaper if mist is not available and the weather is sunny and hot. Make sure the compost does not dry out, but do not over water. Borage,

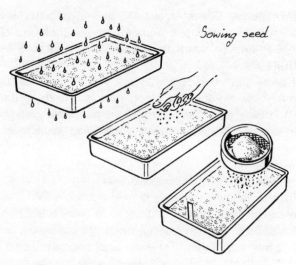

Sowing seed

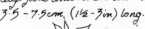

Soft cuttings - cut below node or leaf joint and remove lower leaves. 3.5 - 7.5 cm. (1½-3in) long.

Pelargonium cuttings (aromatic)-remove lower leaves.

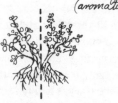

Division - divide clumps using two forks or a knife.

Chervil, Chives, Coriander and Dill are often better sown directly into the retail pot. Square pots are useful for this purpose as they fit closely together on the propagation bed.

Cuttings

Most herbs may be increased by soft 1 in (2–3 cm) cuttings taken from the tip of a new shoot. Always take the cuttings from a strong pest- and disease-free plant that has been watered and fed sufficiently to produce an abundance of cuttings.

Requirements

1. Compost (as for seed compost).
2. Sharp clean knife – learn how to sharpen it safely!
3. Containers for cuttings. There are many types available; the sectional ones are most useful where the plants are separated from each other. The extra-large ones are tempting, but a standard size which will take 40 or 60 cuttings fits well on a heated bed and avoids wasted space.
4. Bin for rubbish and leaves.
5. Labels. Pen. Notebook for records.
6. Cuttings (keep covered to stop wilting if you cannot use them immediately).
7. Hormone powder. Best to buy in small quantities – it deteriorates.
8. Dish for the hormone powder – never dip cuttings into the containers.
9. Dibber to make holes.

Method   First, fill all the containers with compost, making sure that it is firm at the base, and then fill loosely leaving no air pockets. The compost should be moist, not wet. Cut below a leaf joint on the cutting, strip off the bottom leaves, dip in hormone powder, and insert the cutting into the container using a dibber if necessary. I rarely use hormone powder – but it can help at certain times of the year, or until you build up confidence and speed. (The Agricultural Training Board have an excellent 'speed cutting' course which is worth attending if possible.) Label the container with the name of the plant and the date then place on the heated bed and water. A simple and enjoyable task; everyone likes taking cuttings!

The time taken for roots to develop varies according to the plant and the time of year. Lift and inspect the containers from time to time, and when the roots begin to show through the compost, remove them from the heated bed. 'Wean' them by giving less water for a few days before potting on.

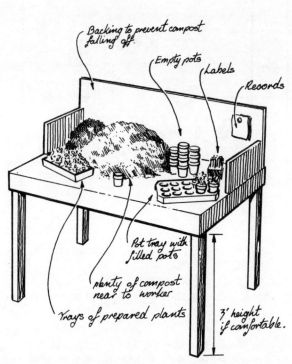

Backing to prevent compost falling off.

Empty pots

Labels

Records

Pot tray with filled pots

plenty of compost near to worker

Trays of prepared plants

3' height if comfortable.

Pick up pot with right hand, plant with left, pot it, take pot to pot tray with right hand and then pick up next empty pot while left hand picks up plant.

Root Division

A very useful method for increasing Thymes, Origanums, etc –
any plant which spreads and produces multiple stems. Gently
tease the roots apart and repot the resulting small plants in
fresh compost.

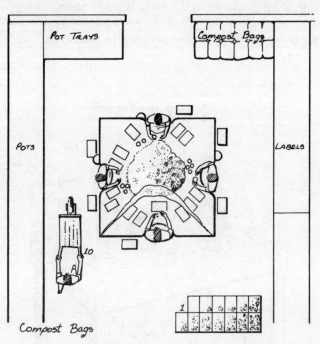

1 Trays of propagated plants for potting.
2 'Dirty' section. Plants are trimmed back if necessary,
pushed out and graded into trays. Rubbish bin
beneath table.
3 Plant is selected with left hand, pot with right hand.
4 Box of pots.
9 Stack of pot trays or boxes to hold pots for moving.
6 Trays of trimmed, prepared plants.

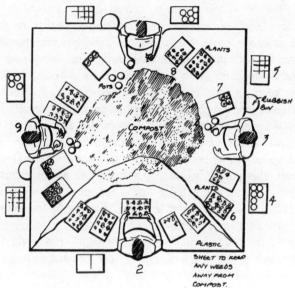

7 Finished plants in trays.

8 Compost near to potter.

9 Right hand puts finished pot in tray and picks up next pot while left hand selects next plant.

10 Flat wheelbarrow to collect and remove finished trays of labelled plants, worker to keep potters 'fed' with pots, trays and plants.

Equipment
Potting Tables Etc.
As a firm believer in the speed-potting system and table designed by ADAS for the Agricultural Training Board, I find it difficult to imagine working with anything else now! The main requirements for potting are: space for trays and pots; a back

board fixed to the bench to retain plenty of compost; the correct height of table for sitting or standing so that the hands and forearms move freely without hunching the shoulders; space beneath the table for rubbish bins and spare pots etc; good lighting; labels to hand in alphabetical order; sufficient door room to allow entrance for a wheelbarrow or trolley to transport finished plants. My potting area is not ideal – but I feel we have made the best use of the space. It is very essential to plan carefully all 'movements' in a repetitive job so that speed can be built up without stress and strain. Dodging round other people, working in a bad light or an uncomfortable position makes one irritable and is not good for the plants!

Think about movement and time. Every time you move a pot or walk a longer distance than necessary it is adding to the cost of the plant (from your point of view). Even when you stand and do nothing it is expensive if you have invested in materials and machinery and they are not constantly in use.

Compost

This is the name given to the blend of ingredients used for propagation and potting. Sterilization is necessary to destroy pests and weed seeds, and the compost should have a stable structure which will retain adequate moisture yet supply good drainage. The particle size is important; the larger air spaces retain air, the small spaces will provide water capacity. Nutrients are taken up by the plant via the water, and air is vital for root health – you wouldn't be very happy with your feet in water all day! Ballast for pot stability is supplied by heavier materials like grit and coarse sand. Materials which may be mixed in various proportions include loam, peat, forest bark, perlite, vermiculite, sand and grit. Fertilizers may be short- or long-term release. Trace elements, lime, pesticides and fungicides may be included to prevent early attack by scarid fly and botrytis etc. The aim is to provide the best possible growing medium which will encourage a good healthy root system resulting in abundant leaf growth and flower development. Excellent leaflets and further information are available from your local Ministry of Agriculture, Fisheries and Food office. For those intending to be organic growers the Soil Association offers advice on alternatives to chemicals (address on page 152).

Potting Compost Each grower has his or her own favourite recipe! I did not feel I needed a compost mixer, nor do I have space for bulk deliveries, so I have the compost made to our own requirements and delivered in bags, 4 cubic metres at a time. This means the compost is 'portable' and potting can take place anywhere on the nursery – it is more sensible to move the compost to the plants for repotting instead of moving plants back and forth from the main potting area. A good proprietary soilless mix is useful to start with. Good loam is becoming increasingly difficult to obtain; peat and composted bark are good alternatives.

Examples of two composts:

1. **Organic:** 50% sphagnum moss peat;
   25% sterilized loam;
   25% grit;
   7 lbs (3.18 kg) Supergro NB organic fertilizer per cubic metre;
   22 gal (100 litres) vermiculite per cubic metre.

Supergro is a 12–14 week slow-release fertilizer. Feed wth Maxicrop or other organic liquid feed after this time.

2. **Inorganic:** 75% medium grade Irish moss peat;
   25% Cambark 100/or sharp sand and grit;
   6.6 lb (3 kg) per cubic metre 9-month slow-release fertilizer.
   55 lb (25 kg) per cubic metre ammonium nitrate if Cambark is used.

How much Compost? Compost is measured in litres – 1,000 litres equals 1 cubic metre. Proprietary makes of compost usually have the volume in litres on the bag.

Type of container	Number filled per 50-litre compost bag	Bags required to fill 1,000
Plastic Pots		
3½ in (9 cm)	370	2.7
4½ in (11.5 cm)	175	5.7
5½ in (14 cm)	98	10.2
9 in (23 cm)	23	42.7
Seed Trays		
1 in (2.5 cm) deep	76	13
2 in (5 cm) deep	38	26

These are approximate amounts. The exact amount of compost required will vary according to the size of plant being potted.

Pots and Carrying Trays

Quite bewildering numbers of new and interesting pots appear each year at the trade shows, with pot trays or carriers designed for easy movement in quantity, or for attractive displays. Round pots are very popular when selling direct to the public, while square pots of a thinner plastic are popular for wholesale work and for holding plants intended for field planting at a later date. It is very much your choice and how much you want to pay. The trade magazines have regular advertisements, and horticultural sundriesmen can show you what is available. It is worth while taking time off to visit shows for the nursery stock trade to compare the merits or disadvantages of various pots. Usually samples will be offered so that you can test them under working conditions.

If you are going to concentrate on herb plant production, carrier trays are essential – these enable you to stand plants neatly and to count accurately.

Standing-out beds

These are areas where your newly potted plants will be able to grow on without check until ready for sale. They may be

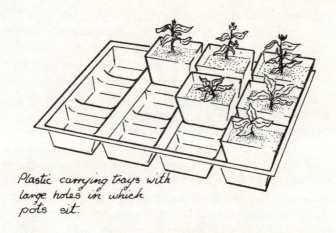

Plastic carrying trays with large holes in which pots sit.

Expanded polystyrene carrying trays with various dimensions for different quantities and sizes of pot.

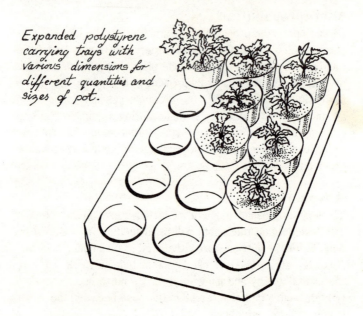

constructed of sand, gravel or woven plastic all of which suppress weeds and allow drainage of excess water. Kill all perennial and annual weeds with a contact herbicide and put down slug bait before making any new standing space. (With organic growers, newspaper, black polythene and 'slug traps' are popular.) It is usually easier to water herb pots by overhead irrigation – sprinklers if you have them, hose pipe and spray if the area is not too large.

A seed tray of 60 cuttings will require 8 to 10 times the area of the seed tray, when potted and standing out. Measure how many seed trays will fit on your propagation bed, multiply by this figure and you can estimate the amount of standing-out bed required. (The idea being to avoid propagating more plants than you can stand out.) Do leave paths between 'blocks' of plants so that you can remove them easily when required.

Micropropagation

Should space for propagation of small plants be limited, it is now possible to obtain several varieties of herbs that have multiplied by cloning from a single plant. Many of these have proved their worth by rapidly growing into good-looking plants for early summer sales. It is usually necessary to order in advance so that a delivery is made during a suitable week in early spring. This method provides great scope for planning the potting operation and scheduling for your own advance order sales.

Aftercare

The length of the active life of the fertilizer used in the compost will decide when the plants will need feeding; this should be done *before* the nutrients are exhausted using a liquid fertilizer. A not-too-strong mixture used once or twice a week will keep the plants healthy and growing well. I tend to use a seaweed type through a dilutor inserted in the hose between the water supply and the sprinklers.

During the early part of the season, potted-up plants in polytunnels may need protection from too much heat, by the use of mesh ventilation at the sides of the tunnel. This will prevent heat build-up on a sunny day (see illustration on page 18). Later in the spring, shade may be necessary for plants which 'bolt' into flower in hot situations, eg Chervil, Parsley.

Trimming back after flowering will help to keep the plants bushy. Never let herbs grow thin and straggly – and, of course, weeds should not be competing for space in the pots! Look around the nursery for neglected corners and edges where weeds have proliferated – their seeds can travel quite a distance on a windy day.

Labels

These are essential for yourself and your customers. Memory is unreliable – once you have muddled different varieties of unlabelled lavender plants for instance, there is a year to wait for flowering and re-sorting if they are of similar growth habit! Depending on the number of plants grown, labelling methods may vary from the patiently hand-written ones (a winter evening's task) to the sophisticated hot-foil-printed, weather-proof types bearing the nursery name and your own information on the particular plant. Computer-produced labels are becoming very popular, and will last through a season and the following winter before needing renewal. For any type of label, the information should be accurate and informative: English and Latin name, mature height, flower colour, and if possible something about the plant and its uses. Picture labels are attractive but do check them for accuracy. Sometimes the picture and name do not match. The names of suppliers of many types of labels are given on page 157.

Labels seem to be a great expense when first ordered. If however you relate the cost of the label to the value of the finished pot and the influence that label may have upon an intending purchaser, they are worth every penny.

Specimen Plants

Even if you are producing only your first few hundred plants, it is worth while to select some of the best to grow on in larger containers or polybags. I have already mentioned the value of stock plants, which can be brought into warmth during the winter to obtain early cuttings for propagation. Once you have a surplus of large plants and you become known to other growers, you will find that at times of disaster – polytunnels blowing away in freak winds etc – this reservoir of good large plants is invaluable. Over the past years I have sold many large plants to friends within the herb trade who have had to rebuild their basic stock. After all – how are you going to start building up yours?

Hints for good basic nursery practice

Large or small nursery, back garden or hectares of land, there are certain quite practical and common-sense rules that you can apply, which save time and prevent small problems turning into disasters!

Ensure that there is cleanliness and tidiness everywhere. I do not mean neatly stacked peat bales waiting for the quiet time for moving them to their appointed place, but the general 'look' of the nursery. Tools should not be left out to deteriorate, wheelbarrows should have a permanent home so that it is always easy to find one. Unwound string lines are a safety hazard, and if left in the soil are almost impossible to extract from cultivators. Piles of weeds waiting for 'someone' to remove them are unsightly as are seed boxes and pots stacked at angles and liable to fall over. All these things create a bad impression. It is all too easy, when you are busy, for tidying up to become too large a job, and as a result the general appearance of the nursery is not good.

Keep water butts, compost for potting, sand and peat, covered – it's amazing how many weed seeds will find their way into these items anyway. No need to give an open invitation! Try to keep paths and doorways clear – it may be you who will fall over on a dark night! Watch out for slippery surfaces on regularly-used paths. Put down sand if necessary in hazardous conditions. Think about creating comfortable working positions at benches and potting tables when doing essential but lengthy routine jobs; it will help create speed with efficiency. Wear the right clothing, it should be wind and weather proof. Thermal underwear and fingerless gloves are invaluable in the winter as are good boots with cosy socks and a hat to keep the head warm. I look formidable in my tweed trilby but it is more comfortable than a woolly hat or headscarf. In summer, of course, clothes are much easier. Even so, if you are dressed suitably and comfortably for the job, you feel more able to achieve the state of mind to enjoy doing a task well. It's called job satisfaction!

4
Herb plant nurseries

Personal temperament plays a major part when making the decision whether to run a retail or wholesale plant nursery. Enjoying conversation, helping new gardeners, advising on garden design and explaining about the virtues of herbs are all part of the day when dealing with the general public. Too much self-selection of plants and obediently queuing at a check-out till without discussion does not fit in with herb magic at all! If you feel impatient with customers it will show – and then how do you imbue your staff with confidence and knowledge if you dislike dealing with the endless string of daily questions yourself?

For someone who loves to concentrate on the growing of herb plants, and has good organizing ability, then the production of small or larger plants to sell wholesale to garden centres and retail nurseries may be an attractive proposition. The income from this tends to be seasonal but this is common to the entire nursery stock trade.

Often the names of nurseries reflect their friendly attitude, so think carefully before you christen your enterprise and imagine how it will sound in ten years' time! J.R. Brown, Herb Plants sounds very businesslike and wholesale. Brown's Garden Centre covers a multitude of items from fish ponds to wire-netting supports as well as plants. Brown's Herb Centre – to live up to this, you need to make sure you have everything from dried herbs, posters and pot pourri, to vast ranges of herb plants and a good fund of knowledge.

Retail Nursery
Layout
Already in Chapter 2 I have discussed the subject of car parking and adequate access to the nursery, also the need for market research to find the customer potential in your area, and how well it is already supplied with herb plants. A small point about car parks – it is wise to have as large an area as is practical within the available space. During the quieter months of the year when only a few cars are parked, it can look somewhat depressing, but you can always reduce the space with clever displays of herbs in containers, portable plant barrows or tables – anything that will catch the eye and make people ignore the empty space!

Once the cars are parked, and people wander in – how do you welcome them (I don't mean personally!)? Most new and curious customers need information – where do they go, where is everything? So you need to give some thought to what is known as 'flow pattern'. Forget the fact that you could find your way around the nursery blindfold and put yourself in the position of a customer. Walk through the main entrance and look carefully to see where simple direction signs should be sited. Don't make them too long and complicated; in my experience very few people read more than can be taken in at the first glance. Even a simple arrow system is better than a notice covered in small print – many people wear spectacles, and many more need them but forget to bring them!

Now you are following your signs. Where do they lead – past a view of an untidy compost heap? So often growers are used to seeing and ignoring important but unattractive areas of their nurseries, oblivious of the fact that a new customer looks at *everything*.

Are the plants laid out in a clear plan? I can't suggest the ideal one, we seem to do some replanning every year. The alphabetical system breaks down when it is too early for half-hardy plants, and what does one do with all the inevitable

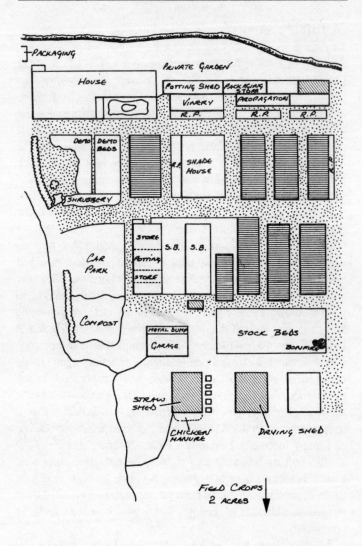

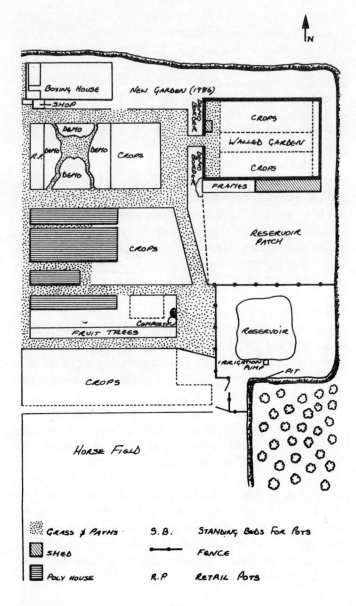

'extras' that have been forgotten in the first flush of enthusiasm at the beginning of the season, not to mention the newly acquired treasures in August! The absolute newcomers to herbs require a simple collection; life-long enthusiasts are looking for additions to their large herb gardens. The husband of one keen herb gardener on her first visit to us was found sitting in his car saying it was 'all too much for him to take in!' The lesson to me was to break down groups of plants into more easily digestible portions.

The following point also may seem obvious, but it is worth mentioning – don't put attractive displays at places where you will get a bottleneck of people standing in admiration. Shaped displays, where in theory customers walk round in the same direction, should be avoided. Someone always starts at the wrong end and people become trapped while others pass by. If you watch a crowd from a height it is fascinating how each individual unconsciously retains his or her own personal space around them.

Labels and back labels on beds

These are most important, especially during the early and late seasons. I find it hard to recognize some plants in their early stages, so obviously the customers need to feel convinced they are buying the right plant. Individual labels are most important. I always feel faintly uneasy when buying plants for myself from a general nursery where there are few labels, especially if the person serving me dithers a bit before writing the label on the spot. It is so easy to be hurried, and this can result in both wrong spelling and naming, which is then perpetuated.

Prices

Some clear method of pricing is necessary; the sale of good plants may be lost if the customer gets tired of constantly having to find 'someone' to price them. Not everyone has a bottomless purse and a limit may have been set to the sum to be expended on plant purchases. Customers should leave the nursery happy with their new plants, not embarrassed because

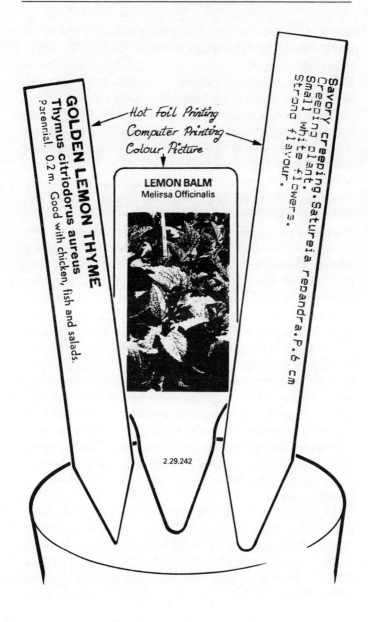

Hot Foil Printing
Computer Printing
Colour Picture

GOLDEN LEMON THYME
Thymus citriodorus aureus
Perennial. 0.2 m. Good with chicken, fish and salads.

LEMON BALM
Melissa Officinalis

2.29.242

Savory creeping.
Creeping plant.
Small white flowers.
Strong flavour. Satureia repandra.P.6 cm

they have spent too much, or had to discard a few when paying. Pricing is discussed more fully in Chapter 8.

Where do they pay?

Or shall I rephrase this question – where do you receive the reward for your hard work? Don't gloss over the fact that while you, of course, are thoroughly enjoying working with plants, you are also actually doing it to earn some money! If you were not really interested in some profit you would not have been intrigued enough to read this far. It is strange how many people are embarrassed about taking money. I have seen everything from rusty tins in the corner of a greenhouse, the grower's pockets, cardboard boxes, to the other extreme – flashing, pinging, multi-point tills. Dignify the procedure a little and show the customers that you value their money. Use a reasonable cash tin (with plenty of change). You should have some idea what float was in the till or cash tin at the beginning of the day, otherwise how can you assess results at the day's end? Also a crowd of people does not necessarily mean a good cash flow – so if there isn't, why not? Are you selling – or have you sold out of the plants most in demand?

Collecting baskets

How are your customers to collect the plants as they select them, and how are they to take them home? Everyone finds their own solution to this: wire baskets, trugs, cardboard punnets with handles; look around and use your ingenuity to see what containers are discarded in your area. The busy local greengrocer's is a good place to look, and usually he is quite pleased to have his empty boxes collected.

Opening times

If you are working alone, it is wise to think carefully about the times and days you will be open for customers. Otherwise it could be almost impossible to get the necessary everyday work completed. When you are seen to be working on your plants, even when the nursery is closed, it will still be assumed that you are free to sell a few plants and have an hour's chat at the same time 'while you are not busy'. I love meeting and talking to new people about herbs – but not at all hours of the day and evening.

Catalogues

These become more glossy and 'up market' every year. Don't feel it is necessary to spend a fortune on printing bills until you are sufficiently established to live up to a glossy image. Nothing is worse than to travel to visit some place with an amazing list of plants and find it does not fulfil its promise. I remember getting quite excited about a friend's new plant list, only to be informed that the plants would be available only if and when the seeds germinated – and not many were making the effort!

How do you look?

Having burnished up your nursery, what about your own appearance? It may seem a rather personal note to raise, but how cheerful are you? 'Smile though your heart is breaking' may sound trite, but the customer is not really interested in your domestic or financial problems, unless he's also an old friend or relative. He is there to buy plants and a sloppy appearance together with a dismal face will not give him much encouragement.

Wholesale Nursery

Perhaps the thought of dealing with the public en masse does not appeal, and anyway your nursery is not situated where there are likely to be prospective customers. Before growing thousands of plants do find and research the potential market. Garden centres, retail nurseries, field crop growers – all require plants grown in large numbers at a price which will give them sufficient financial returns either as a retail 'mark up' or in yields from crops. Transport of plants will have to be considered either by carrier or by your own van. Carrying trays and safe stacking or boxing are essential if the delivery is to arrive in good condition.

When costing and setting the wholesale prices, customer requirements have to be taken into consideration and some form of forward ordering system devised that will not alarm the customer, but enable you to plan the number of plants to propagate. Regular delivery is usually necessary for larger garden centres and even some form of merchandising advice on caring for the plants if they hang about unsold and begin to look neglected.

Mail Order Plants

This can be more seasonal than other methods of selling plants. Who knows what actually impels someone unseen and unknown to you to actually pick up a pen and fill out an order form? Even if you feel you have an offer of plants which is really 'different' and should have wide appeal, you can never gauge the response until the orders do or don't flow in!

Advertising in the gardening press, local and national gardening columns seems to have produced a steady small trade for some growers. Producing for a special 'offer' in a magazine or postal catalogue can bring disastrously poor results or alarmingly big orders. One that I did with a national society in their postal magazine appeared on the same day as a certain other consumer magazine produced a survey condemning mail order herbs. I didn't appear in the survey I'm pleased to say, but it didn't do much for the carefully thought out postal offer for which I'd planned and propagated for months.

Postal packing is more lightweight and sophisticated these days, expanded polystyrene packs in all shapes and plant-holding amounts being now available. Cardboard box packs must be waterproof and not liable to collapse. The Post Office takes objection to bits of soil shaking out on to the other mail!

A herb is now generally defined to be a plant, which may, in some of its parts, be beneficial to man. It can be the root, stem, bark, leaf, flower or fruit. I would also include the aromatic properties.

This is such a general definition that there are thousands of plants which could be considered for selling in a true herb nursery. In practice about two hundred species and varieties are commonly requested during the year, although one may stock five hundred or more altogether. The following plant table is intended to be of assistance to the new grower of the herbs that are popular with the public. The effect of a popular gardening programme or magazine article cannot be underestimated – anything from Coltsfoot to Self Heal may suddenly seem desirable – and people will come for miles in search of a recommended plant.

The chart is based on experience of the climate in south-east England. There will be variations in different areas.

Abbreviations.
A = Annual,
B = Biennial,
P = Perennial,
HH = Half hardy.

* = Expected to be stocked, but varying popularity

Plant	Propagation	Remarks	Popularity
Alecost (Costmary), P *Chrysanthemum balsamita*	division, cuttings	Silvery leaf, aromatic	●
Alexanders, P *Smyrnium olusatrum*	seed, division	Also called black lovage	*
Angelica, B *Angelica archangelica*	Drill seed when ripe	Large graceful plant	●●●
Anise, A *Pimpinella anisum*	seed	Aromatic seeds and leaves	●●●
Anise Hyssop, P *Agastache anethiodora*	seed, cuttings	Very attractive purple flower spikes	●●●
Artemisias **Mugwort**, P *Artemisia vulgaris*	seed, cuttings	Silver grey leaves, reddish stems	*
Roman Wormwood, P *Artemisia pontica*	cuttings	Aromatic fronds, silver green foliage	●●
Southern- wood, P *Artemisia abrotanum*	cuttings	Cut back each spring to produce green bush	●●
Wormwood, P *Artemisia absinthium* See also Tarragon, French p.63	cuttings	Fine silver leaves	●

Plant	Propagation	Remarks	Popularity
Balm, Lemon, P *Melissa officinalis*	seed, division	Rapid growth, lemon-scented leaves	●
variegated form	cuttings	Very pretty gold/green variegation	●●●
Basil *Ocimum*			
Bush, HHA *Ocimum minimum*	seed	Small leaf, neat plant	●●
Purple (Red), HHA *Ocimum basilicum purpurea*	seed	Rich purple leaves	●●●●
Sweet, HHA *Ocimum basilicum*	seed	Large very aromatic leaves	●●●●
Bay (Noble Laurel), P *Laurus nobilis*	seed, cuttings	Always in demand	●●●
Bergamot, P *Monarda didyma*	seed, cuttings, division	Red, pink, white or purple	●●●
Borage, A *Borago officinalis*	seed	Bright blue flowers	●●
Box, P *Buxus sempervirens*	cuttings	Slow growth hedging plant	*
Bugle, P *Ajuga reptans*	cuttings, division	Ground cover, many colours of leaf	●●
Burnet, **Salad**, P *Poterium sanguisorba*	seed, division	Green leaves throughout winter	*
Camphor Plant, P *Balsamita vulgaris*	cuttings, division	Silver leaf, yellow flower	●
Caraway, B *Carum carvi*	seed	Culinary	*

Plant	Propagation	Remarks	Popularity
Catmint, P *Nepeta mussini*	seed, cuttings	Blue flowers, grey leaves	●●●
Catnip, P *Nepeta cataria*	seed	Loved by cats, grey leaves	●
Chamomile			

Dyer's, P
  Anthemis
  tinctoria
	seed,
	division
		Bright yellow
		flowers
			●

German, A
  Matricaria
  recutita
	seed	Becomes rather
		straggly in pots
			*

Roman, P
  Anthemis nobilis,
  (syn *cham-*
  aemelum nobile)
	seed,
	division,
	cuttings
		Creamy single
		or double
		flowers, ground
		cover
			●●●

'Treneague', P
  Anthemis nobilis
  treneague
	division,
	cuttings
		Non-flowering
		ground cover
			●●●

Chervil, A *Anthriscus cerefolium*	seed	Culinary	●●
Comfrey, P *Symphytum* *officinale*	root division	Bold plant, requires large container	●●
Chive/Onion Family, *Allium Cepa*			

Chives, P
  Allium
  schoenoprasum
	seed,
	division
		Purple/pink
		flowers
			●●●

Garlic, P *Allium sativum*	best grown as sets	Popular but difficult to retain in pots	●
Garlic Chives, P *Allium tuberosum*	seed, division	Gentle, garlic flavour and pretty white flowers	●●
Tree Onion, P *Allium profilerum*	seed, division	Onion bulbs cluster on top of long stalks	*

Plant	Propagation	Remarks	Popularity
Welsh Onion, P *Allium fistulosum*	seed, division	Dramatic round flower heads	●
Coriander, A *Coriandrum sativum*	seed	Grows rapidly and needs frequent reseeding in pots to look attractive	●●●
Cotton Lavender, P *Santolina* *Santolina chamaecyparissus* *Santolina neopolitana*	cuttings "	Very attractive grey or silvery leaf plants, yellow or creamy button flowers	●●●
Santolina serratifolia virens		Grey/green serrated foliage, low growing	●
Santolina viridis		Deep green foliage.	●
Cowslip, P *Primula veris*	seed, division	Very popular when in flower	●
Cumin, A *Cuminum cyminum*	seed	Culinary, not sold in large quantities	*
Curry Plant, P *Helichrysum serotinum* syn. *H. angustifolium*	cuttings	Silver leaves, yellow flower	●●●●
Curry Plant, Dwarf, P *Helichrysum italicum*	cuttings	Tiny silver leaves and buds	●●●●
Dill, A *Anethum graveolens*	seed	Culinary. Feathery leaves, yellow flowerheads	●●●

Plant	Propagation	Remarks	Popularity
Elecampane, P *Inula helenium*	seed, division	Stately large plant, yellow flower heads	●
Evening Primrose, B *Oenothera biennis*	seed	Primrose yellow flowers open daily up the stem	●
Fennel, Sweet, P *Foeniculum vulgare dulce*	seed	Leaves rich green. Also bronze-leaf variety, yellow flowers	●●●
Fennel, Florence, A *Foeniculum vulgare* *(Finocchio)*	seed	Swollen base of leaves used as vegetable	*
Feverfew, P *Chrysanthemum parthenium* (syn. *tanacetum parthenium*)	seed, cuttings	Green or gold leaf varieties, single or double flowers	●●●
Foxglove, B *Digitalis purpurea* (& Hybrids)	seed	White, rose or purple flowers	●
Goat's Rue (French Lilac), P *Galega officinalis*	seed, division	Attractive sweet pea type flowers, blue or white. Rapid growth	●
Golden Rod, P *Solidago virgaurea*	seed, division	Treat as herbaceous plant	●
Heartsease (Wild Pansy), A/P *Viola tricolor*	seed, layering	Free flowering minute 3 coloured 'faces'. Best in first year	●●
Hops, Green or Gold, P *Humulus lupulus*	cuttings	Rapid climber, female required for 'hops'. Gold variety very decorative	●●● ●●●

Plant	Propagation	Remarks	Popularity
Horehound, White, P *Marrubium vulgare*	seed, cuttings	Greyish woolly aromatic leaves	*
Horseradish, P *Armoracia rusticana*	root division	Needs large pots	●●●●
Houseleek, P *Sempervivum tectorum*	division	Fat clumps, succulent leaves.	*
Hyssop, P *Hyssopus officinalis*	seed, cuttings	Blue, white, pink or purple flowers	●●●●
Hyssop, Rock, P *Hyssopus aristatus*	cuttings	Rich blue flowers, bushy habit	●●●●
Jacob's Ladder, P *Polemonium caeruleum*	seed, division	Showy blue or white flowers	●●
Jerusalem Sage, P *Phlomis fructicosa*	cuttings	Tender in harsh weather	●
Juniper *Juniperus communis*	cuttings, seed	Requires male and female plants for berries	●●●
Lady's Bedstraw, P *Galium verum*	seed, division	Name always attracts attention	*
Lady's Mantle, P *Alchemilla mollis*	seed, division	Needs large containers to show to best advantage	●●
Lavender, P *Lavendula officinalis* syn. *'Vera')* Some popular varieties	cuttings, not always true from seed	Many varieties and colours, always popular	●●●●
Hidcote Blue *L. nana* *atropurpurea*	Cuttings, not always true from seed.	Silvery foliage, deep mauve-blue flowers	●●●●

Plant	Propagation	Remarks	Popularity
Munstead *L. angustifolia*	"	Soft green leaf, mauve flowers	●●●●
Pink (usually Lodden Pink) *L. rosea*	"	Pale pink flowers	●●●●
Royal purple *L. officinalis*	"	Rich purple flowers	●●●●
'Vera' *L. officinalis*	"	Vigorous silvery foliage, pale mauve flowers, strong-scented	●●●●
'French' *L. stoechas*	"	Unusual flowers	●●●●
Lovage, P *Levisticum officinale*	seed, division	Increasing in popularity	●
Lungwort, P *Pulmonaria officinalis*	seed, division	Dark green leaves with white spots. Spring flowers of pink/blue	●●●
Mace, P *Achillea decolorans*	seed, division	Cream, daisy-type flowers. Hot spicy flavour	*
Marigold, A *Calendula officinalis*	seed	Well-known original type with double or single orange flowers with dark centre	●
Marjoram Many varieties & hybrids	cuttings, division	All very popular and attractive	
Compact Marjoram, P *Origanum compactum*		Very pretty pink flowers. Good edging plant	●●●●
Golden Marjoram, P *Origanum vulg. aureum* (many different forms)		Requires shade. Curly-leaved types less liable to scorch	●●●●

Plant	Propagation	Remarks	Popularity
Pot Marjoram, P *Origanum onites*		Tall long-lasting flowers of pink-purple	●●●
Oregano (Wild Marjoram), P *Origanum vulgare*		Strongest flavour. Usually has white flowers	●●●●
Sweet Marjoram (Knotted Marjoram), HHP *Origanum majorana*	seed	Silky-grey, sweet-scented leaves, white knots of flowers Usually grown as annual	●
Madder Dyer's, P *Rubia tinctorium*	seed, division	'Sticky' rapid sprawling growth	*
Marshmallow, P *Althaea officinalis*	seed	Grey-green leaves, delicate pink flowers	●
Meadowsweet, P *Filipendula ulmaria*	seed, division	Fragrant, creamy-white flower plumes	*
Melilot, B *Melilotus officinalis*	seed	Rapid growth. Yellow or white flowers	*
Mint, P **Apple Mint**, P *M. rotundifolia* syn. *M. suaveolens*	seed, cuttings, division	Apple-scented	●
Bowles Mint, P *M. rotundifolia* (Bowles var)	cuttings, division	Apple-scented, tail growth	●●●
Corsican Mint, P *M. requienii*	division	Tiny purple flowers. Looks well if flowing over pot	●●●●

Plant	Propagation	Remarks	Popularity
Eau-de-Cologne Mint, P *Mentha piperata × citrata*	cuttings, division	Also called orange, lemon, bergamot, lavender mint according to slight changes in aromatic oil content	●●
Ginger Mint, P *Mentha × gentilis variegata*	cuttings, division	Needs regular trimming to look well	●●●
Pennyroyal, P *Mentha pulegium*	cuttings, seed, rooted offsets	Upright and creeping forms	●●●
Peppermint, Black, P *Mentha × piperita*	cuttings, division	Select for rich dark colour, and clear peppermint scent	●●●
Pineapple Mint, P *M. rotundifolia variegata*	cuttings, division	Very attractive white or cream variegations	●●●●
Spearmint (Garden mint) P *Mentha × spicata (Viridis)*	cuttings, division	Select for rust resistance and clear scent	●●●●
Motherwort, P *Leonurus cardiaca*	seed, division	Sells well in larger containers	*
Mullein, B *Verbascum thapsus*	seed	Grey woolly leaves, yellow flowers	*
Myrtle, P *Myrtus communis*	cuttings, seed	Tall, dwarf and variegated forms	●●●
Nasturtium, A *Tropaeolum majus*	seed	Many colours and habits	●●●●
Orris, P *Iris florentina*	division	White/pale mauve flowers	●●

Plant	Propagation	Remarks	Popularity
Parsley Curled, B *Petroselinum* *crispum*	seed	Flat leaf continental parsley also good Curled leaf always popular, large pots keep good appearance	●●●●
Pasque Flower, P *Pulsatilla vulgaris*	seed	Both flower and seed are attractive	●●
Periwinkle, P Lesser, *vinca minor* Greater, *vinca major*	cuttings, division	Green and variegated forms	●
Primrose, P *Primula vulgaris*	seed, division	Late summer potting gives good spring flowers	●●
Pyrethrum, P *Chrysanthemum* *cineriifolium*	seed	White daisy flower strong insecticide	*
Rocket, Sweet, B *Hesperis matronalis* (Dames violet)	seed	Sweet scented mauve or white flowers	●●
Rosemary, P *Rosmarinus* *officinalis*	cuttings	Many attractive varieties. Most popular Miss Jessup upright, lavandulaceous, and all deep blues	●●●●
Rue, P *Ruta graveolens*	seed, cuttings	Jackman's Blue and variegated forms	●●●●
Sage, P *Salvia officinalis*	seed, cuttings	Pink, blue, white or mauve flowers	●●●
Narrow Leaf, P	seed	Good shades of colours. Stands winter well	●●

Plant	Propagation	Remarks	Popularity
Broad Leaf, P (Rarely flowers)	cuttings	Low growth habit, attractive soft grey leaves Useful when narrow leaf is flowering	●●
Clary Sage, B *Salvia sclarea*	seed	Large colourful flower bracts	●●
Golden, P *S. officinalis icterina*	cuttings	Soft gold green variegated	●●●●
'Painted', A *S. horminum*	seed	Purple or pink bracts	*
Pineapple, P *S. rutilans*	cuttings	Red flowers, good winter house plant	●●
Red (purple) P. *S. officinalis purpurascens*	cuttings	Rich blue flower	●●●●
Tricolor, P *S. officinalis tricolor*	cuttings	Can be tender. Pinch back early to bush out	●●●●
Savory Summer, A *Satureja hortensis*	seed	Pinky flowers, purple stems	●●
Winter, P *Satureja montana*	seed, cuttings	Pinky white flowers	●●●
Creeping, P *Satureja repandra*	seed, cuttings	White flowers, creeping habit	●●
Soapwort, P *Saponaria officinalis*	seed, division	Lovely pink flowers. Double form available	●
Sorrel, large leaf, P *Rumex acetosa*	seed, division	Type usually required for culinary use	●●●
Sorrel small leaf, P *Rumex scutatus*	seed, division	Good ground cover. Looks good in pots	●

Plant	Propagation	Remarks	Popularity
Stachys, P *Lanata* (many country names eg Lambs' ears)	division, cuttings	Large silver downy leaves and flower spikes	●
Stonecrop, P *Sedum Acre*	division	Brilliant yellow flowers, needs potting in good time to look at best	●
Sweet Cicely, P *Myrrhis odorata*	seed, division	Fern-like leaves, white flowers	●●●
Tansy, P *Tanacetum vulgare*	seed, division	Decorative, ferny leaves, yellow button flowers Curled leaf form good in pots	●
Tarragon French, P *Artemisia* *dracunculus*	cuttings, division	Keep trimmed to retain bushy plant	●●●●
Thrift, P *Armeria maritima*	seed, division	Cushions of leaves, pink flowers	●
Thymes, P	mainly from cuttings	Many popular varieties, difficult to give a definitive list	●●●●
Broad leaf, *Thymus* *pulegioides* **Culinary** *Thymus vulgaris* **Lemon**, *Thymus vulgaris* *citriodorus*	division		

Examples of upright vars. 'Silver Posie', Golden Lemon,
fragrantissimus, odoratissimus, porlock.

Plant	Propagation	Remarks	Popularity
Many creeping varieties, e.g. *Albus, azoricus, cocineus,* creeping lemon, *deofleri,* 'Doone Valley', *drucei, herba barona* the list seems endless and depends on personal preference and space available			
Valerian, Red ('Untidy Betty'), P *Centranthus ruber*	seed, division	Showy red flowers over long season	●●●
Valerian, P *Valeriana officinalis*	seed	Umbels of pale pink flowers	●●
Verbena, Lemon, HHP *Aloysia triphylla (Lippia citriodora)*	cuttings	Very aromatic leaves	●●●●
Violet, Sweet, P *Viola odorata*	layers, division	Violet or white flowers in spring	●
Wallflower, Wild, B *Cheiranthus cheiri*	seed	Popular if in flower. Deep-rooted so not very good in pots	●
Woad, B *Isatis tinctoria*	seed	Yellow flowers, blue/black seeds	●
Woodruff, Sweet, P *Asperula odorata*	seed, division	Shiny leaves, white star-shaped flowers	●●●

5
Fresh-cut culinary herbs

The thought of providing fresh culinary herbs to chefs and restaurants is foremost in the minds of people who enjoy growing and using herbs in their own cooking. It is not always easy to find fresh herbs in supermarkets and greengrocers, beyond the usual packs of Parsley, Mint and Sage, and so the automatic assumption is that they are not available. If you think more deeply about why a wide range of culinary herbs is not available, then some of the reasons begin to emerge.

Although the general public is becoming very aware of the benefits of using fresh culinary herbs, they do not necessarily make them an essential item on the shopping list. Keen home cooks with gardens grow their own herbs during the summer months, and advice is given constantly in cooking pages and books on how to dry, freeze or preserve herbs in oil for use in the winter. Supermarkets and shops place a definite earning value on shelf space, and herbs at present are fairly low on the priority rating. The amount of herbs you actually see in the supermarkets, shops and wholesale markets represents just the tip of a large iceberg.

Chefs in restaurants and hotels are requiring greatly increased amounts and varieties of culinary herbs, and many chefs now have their own suppliers or their own herb gardens, providing high standards. I feel that new herb growers determined to grow fresh herbs 'for chefs' should be realistic, and not imagine that all one has to do is grow them, and all will be well because 'everyone wants fresh herbs'! A number of large users are already obtaining them from a variety of sources.

One of the other problems of growing for the fresh market is the requirement for continuity of supply, there are always times when the plants do not wish to oblige. It is very easy to grow clumps of Chives as we all know, but to provide fresh Chives week after week for as long as possible is not quite so simple.

Supermarkets need to be supplied on a regional or national basis to make the investment in labour, machinery and administration worthwhile. The main wholesale markets are quite a challenge, but the volume and variety required, and the chance of unsold produce or low financial returns, can make growing for them on a regular basis quite a daunting proposition.

The last thing I would wish to do is to depress keen plantsmen who wish to undertake growing and cutting fresh herbs. We do need more good growers to help supply the increase in demand for all herb products. The advice I have already given and now reiterate is: FIRST FIND AND THEN RESEARCH YOUR MARKET. Start in a fairly small way while you are gaining experience in growing, cutting, packing and delivering. No one can give you a blueprint on how to do it, or how much to grow. Markets, soil, situation differ widely, also the amount of money, energy and time you are prepared to devote. Very few herb farms in England make a total living out of growing fresh herbs, and the importation of herbs has to be organized to fill the off-season gap. It is therefore wise to have another, more stable income .to support you while developing sufficient plants and experience. The fresh-cut herb trade is fascinating but very volatile, and once cut, herbs must be sold while at their best, even though 'shelf life' can be extended by good packaging.

One of the other problems to contend with is the increasing competition from good (and bad), imported herbs. The world is shrinking as transport and cooling become faster and more sophisticated. Kenya, Cyprus, Italy, France, Germany, Holland and now Spain export herbs, and I have even had a consignment offered from New Zealand.

The Demand

Research into local farmshops, restaurants, hotels and organically grown vegetable shops should produce customers who are willing to place steady orders for fresh locally grown herbs. Once your reputation and skill grow then orders will begin to flow in from all directions.

Herbs most in demand (alphabetically)
Basil, large sweet (*Ocimum basilicum*)
Bay leaves (*Laurus nobilis*)
Chervil (*Anthriscus cerefolium*)
Chives (*Allium schoenoprasum*)
Dill (*Anethum graveolens*)
Fennel (*Foeniculum vulgare*)
Marjoram, pot (*Origanum onites*)
Mint (*Mentha viridis*)
Oregano (*Origanum vulgare*)
Parsley, curled (*Petroselinum crispum*)
Rosemary (*Rosmarinus officinalis*)
Sage (*Salvia officinalis*)
Sorrel (*Rumex acetosa*)
Spearmint (*Mentha spicata*, or *M. viridis*)
Tarragon, French (*Artemisia dracunculus*)
Thyme (*Thymus vulgaris*)

Of these, Basil, Chives, Dill and French Tarragon are 'musts' – Garlic (*Allium sativum*) is generally ordered by chefs from their fruit and vegetable wholesalers, and it is in plentiful supply in several varieties, all year round.

Herbs required in smaller quantities
Borage (*Borago officinalis*)
Coriander (*Coriandrum sativum*)
Lemon Balm (*Melissa officinalis*)
Lovage (*Levisticum officinale*)
Marjoram, sweet or knotted (*Origanum majorana*)
Mint, apple (*Mentha rotundifolia* or *Mentha suaveolens*)
Parsley, flat or French (*Petroselinum*)
Rocket, salad (*Eruca sativa*)
Savory, summer (*Satureia hortensis*)
Savory, winter (*Satureia montana*)
Thyme, lemon (*Thymus citriodorus*)

Herbs occasionally required
Angelica (*Angelica archangelica*)
Burnet, salad (*Poterium sanguisorba*)
Celery leaf (*Apium graveolens*)
Dandelion (*Taraxacum officinale*)
Elder Flower (*Sambucus nigra*)
Horseradish (*Armoracia rusticana*)
Hyssop (*Hyssopus officinalis*)
Marigold (*Calendula officinalis*)
Nasturtium (*Tropaeleum majus*)
Nettle (*Urtica dioica*)
Rue (*Ruta graveolens*)
Sweet Cicely (*Myrrhis odorata*)
Verbena, lemon (*Lippia citriodora*)
Woodruff, sweet (*Asperula odorata*)

There are many other items one may be asked to supply from Juniper berries to Water Lily root, but I feel the foregoing lists should satisfy most customers' requirements.

The size of hotel or restaurant bears no relation to the size of the order which you are likely to receive. A well-known, large London hotel may ask for a hundred pounds' worth of herbs per week, a small restaurant with a superb menu may order almost as much. Yet another, only two packs of herbs.

If I look at any one day's orders, they will range in size from

1 Chef's pack* Chives
1 Chef's pack Dill
to
75 Chef's packs Basil
75 Chef's packs French Tarragon
75 Chef's packs Chervil
3 × 2lb (900g) French Sorrel
5 Chef's packs Oregano
1 bunch Borage
20 Chef's packs Rosemary

Anything up to 154 lb (70 kg) in packs can be ordered for the wholesale markets, and up to 220½ lb (100 kg) in bulk for the catering industry, with perhaps 'one bunch of Coriander' for a local customer, who likes authentic Indian cooking. (You will notice that we work in pounds or kilos, according to our customers' preference; smaller orders are usually in imperial measures while bulk orders are metric. Recipe research kitchens ask for grammes!)

Unless the menu is a 'set' one for a period of time, the amount and type of herbs ordered will fluctuate according to the fresh vegetables and meat in season, and whether the people sampling the cuisine like the dishes. There is no way one can anticipate the demand. The only answer is to grow 'enough' as superbly as possible, then bag or overwrap the herbs in a packaging which protects and extends their life-span as long as possible. If you do have a shortage then your customers will be prepared to wait, or come back to you because of the quality of the herbs you grow and the service offered.

---

*A chef's pack is a polystyrene tray 5 x 8½ in (12.5 x 22cm) overwrapped with stretch film and heat sealed.

The foregoing should give you an idea of the demand to be expected and your next consideration is:

The size of growing area required

For a small number of regular customers about ½ acre (·2ha) would be a good starting point, but would hardly provide more than a pocket-money income. To be really serious about a viable income at least 4 acres (1·6ha) of field land will be needed plus protected land and probably much more, as one needs spare land for fallowing and some rotation of crops. Only experience and your records will be able to tell you how much of a certain herb to grow.

The type of records we keep allow us to estimate how many square metres of each herb to allow for over a season. For example, in June, we harvest 2·2lb (1 kg) of Dill per sq. metre. It takes one person 15 minutes to cut 8·8lb (4 kg) into our standard container. The Dill can be packed in 40 minutes into 4 outer boxes each containing 38 of our market packs. We know that three or four cuts of Dill may be taken over eight weeks before it is allowed to flower for other uses, or cultivated back into the soil, thus clearing the beds for further cropping. (When you reach the chapter on costing, turn back to this page and refresh your memory on some of the details necessary to resolve how much you should charge for your fresh herbs!)

HMSO publishes a very good little book entitled *Culinary and Medicinal Herbs*, with tables at the back giving information on seed size and yield rate per acre/hectare for the main culinary and medicinal herbs (see page 153).

Personally, I find it difficult to visualize hectares or acres of anything, so I divide it all down into sq. metre runs of beds. That way, it seems more manageable and slightly domestic! I do all my calculations with the aid of a metric conversion calculator which cost £12 from *Farmer's Weekly*; so take heart because it's not too complicated!

By now you will probably be wondering why I have not

drawn a neat little plan with all the herbs marked out on their bed systems! There are plenty of well-illustrated books for amateur gardeners giving such plans, but if you have any ideas about actually selling your herbs for profit, you have crossed the borderline and, I hope, will be as professional as possible. If there is a shortage of lettuce in the garden because a certain book indicated too small an area, you don't blame the author – you go and buy a lettuce at the greengrocer's and resolve to grow more next time. Once you are selling your produce the customer expects you to be sufficiently professional to have herbs at your finger tips whenever he telephones with an order. This is why I suggest an experimental year growing all the herbs then cutting, weighing and estimating how much you can produce from a measured area. Then you can go out and capture new customers with the confidence of knowing how much you will need to grow – not forgetting to over-estimate, in order to cover emergencies.

Systems of growing
Beds
In open ground or under protection, the width of bed is usually dictated by your machinery. I find a practical guide is to measure how easily you will be able to reach into the centre of the bed from either path for cutting the herbs. This, after all, is the crucial part of your business, and stretched or uncomfortable cutting positions are difficult to sustain after an hour or more and consequently production slows down. Two to three rows may be drilled or planted within a bed. I prefer two rows in a 2ft 6in. (30 cm) bed so that weeding and hoeing can be easily done along the rows, and also right across the width of the beds.

Herbs suitable for bed systems
Annuals and Biennials. Basil, Borage, Chervil, Chives, Coriander, Dill, Sweet Marjoram, Parsley (flat and curly), Summer Savory.

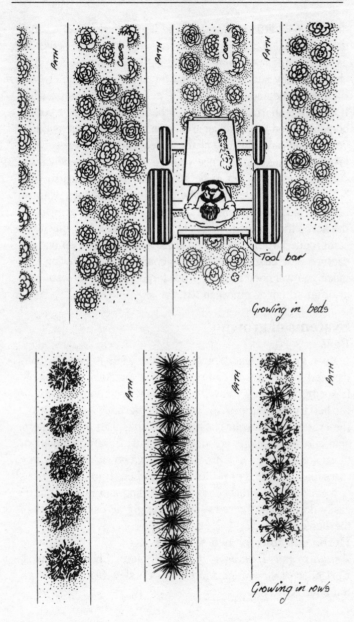

Growing in beds

Growing in rows

Perennials. Chives, Fennel, Marjoram, Oregano, Mints, Rosemary, Sage, Winter Savory, large-leaf Sorrel, French Tarragon, Thymes. (Note: Angelica, Lovage and Melissa are all very large plants and grow well in rows, but have to be sited so that they do not shade sun-loving plants. They can be useful to shade Chervil, which bolts into flower if too exposed in summer.)

Growing in rows (with paths between each single row of plants) This is useful if the space available is limited and the quantity required small. Conversely, it is also useful if large areas are to be used with mechanical weed control. Single rows will give the plants space and lack of competition.

Protected cropping To advance the germination of seedlings by retaining moisture and warmth, rolls of perforated polythene film are now available. Unroll the film down the length of the bed and secure at either end by covering firmly with soil. The sheet of polythene should be laid without too much tension widthways in order to allow the slits in the film to expand as the crop starts to grow. A shallow trench either side of the row, backfilled with soil over the polythene, will hold the edges firmly in place. When all danger of frost has passed, the perforated film should be removed only when the weather is overcast or dull, otherwise the newly exposed tender leaves might be 'scorched' by the full sun. Unfortunately weeds germinate as well so it is advisable to use a contact herbicide (e.g. Gramoxone) a few days before the seed is due to germinate, to 'burn off' the more rapidly germinating weeds. A contact herbicide is a spray solution which will kill on contact all green growth but which rapidly becomes inactive when it reaches the soil.

Low polythene tunnels over wire hoops are useful for early and late season crop protection, having the advantage that the sides can be lifted during the day for ventilation, watering and cropping. The retaining strings hold the polythene firmly in place, but it is still possible to slide the polythene up and down

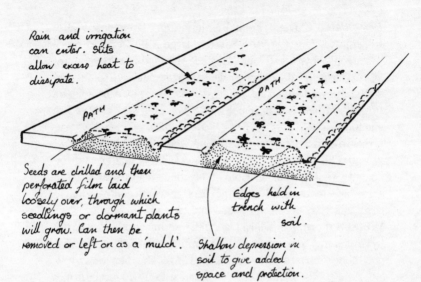

Rain and irrigation can enter. Slits allow excess heat to dissipate.

Seeds are drilled and then perforated film laid loosely over, through which seedlings or dormant plants will grow. Can then be removed or left on as a 'mulch'.

Edges held in trench with soil.

Shallow depression in soil to give added space and protection.

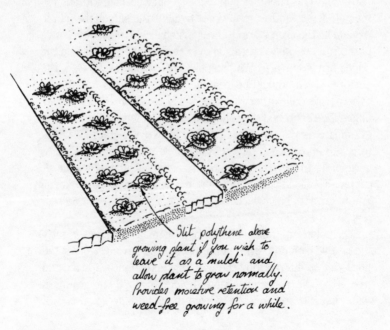

Slit polythene above growing plant if you wish to leave it as a 'mulch' and allow plant to grow normally. Provides moisture retention and weed-free growing for a while.

over the wire hoops as needed. The smooth, not too sharply angled head of a walking stick is useful for 'lifting' the sides and, with practice, a wellie boot with a not too heavy foot inside can be used for closing down long rows. I have clear memories of marching up and down long, polythene rows in the moonlight with my husband, after a frost warning. Sounds romantic, but our total concentration was on left foot forward, right foot ease polythene down, with an occasional not too sweet word when the polythene split!

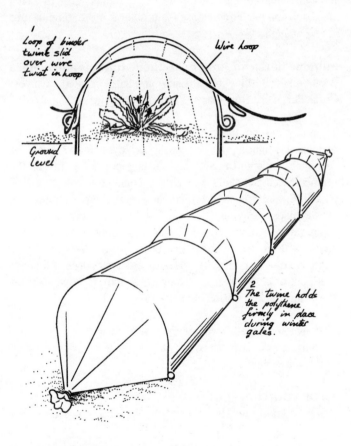

1 Loop of binder twine slid over wire twist in hoop

Wire loop

Ground level

2 The twine holds the polythene firmly in place during winter gales.

Suitable herbs for growing in low polythene tunnels
Basil, Chervil, Chives, Marjoram, Mint, Oregano, Parsley, large-leaf Sorrel, Savory, French Tarragon.

Larger hoops and widths of polythene are available, useful for taller herbs like rosemary, which can be a tender perennial in severe weather. Polythene houses are excellent for many herbs, as long as you keep them well-ventilated, leaving the doors and sides open whenever possible. Even the winter sun can cause high temperatures, with ensuing soft growth which dies back and encourages disease problems if the temperature is low at night.

Suitable herbs for larger polythene tunnels and houses
Basil, Chervil (in winter, early and late season), Chives, Coriander, Dill, Rosemary, French Tarragon.

To really extend the season, soil-warming cables and supplementary lighting are necessary. Never forget that the response of plants to day-length is as important as raising the temperature. Suppliers of lighting equipment are given on page 156, and it is wise to seek advice at the planning stage. Glasshouses provide a more stable, or easily raised, temperature. Many different aids to growing have been designed and are still in the experimental stage; the use of heat pumps and solar energy is currently being explored. All heady stuff, but unless you are an expert, first learn to grow and crop the plants under 'normal' conditions!

The chart on page 52 will give you some help as to when, and by what method, propagation of the most common culinary herbs takes place.

Crop rotation
Always a knotty problem if you have insufficient space to allow

some land to lie fallow (left unused) each year. It affords opportunity for dealing with the problem of perennial weeds, green manuring, and for sub-soiling in order to break up any compacted soil beneath the paths. An additional benefit is the chance to plan for change in the volume and type of herbs grown as the business develops.

Examples of plants which, if they remain healthy and productive, may remain in one situation for years are: Bay, Elder, Lovage, Rosemary, Rue, Sweet Cicely and Woodruff.

Specimens which will require lifting and dividing, or will need new plants from cuttings, every 3–4 years are: Hyssop, Lemon Balm, Marjoram, Oregano, Sage, Salad Burnet, Winter Savory, French Tarragon and Thymes.

The herbs usually grown as biennials (for two seasons) are: Angelica, Celery leaf, Dandelion, Fennel, Parsley (autumn drilled), and large-leaf Sorrel.

Herbs grown from seed as annuals (lasting a single growing season) are: Basil (half hardy), Borage, Chervil, Coriander, Dill, Marigold, Marjoram (sweet), Nasturtium, Parsley and Summer Savory.

Mints are perennials (last three or more seasons). They can be kept in permanent beds if they are of a reasonably rust-free variety, and the weed build-up is not a problem. Clear the beds thoroughly at the end of the season by cutting down and burning all trash. Rust can be a real problem (it manifests itself as rusty-coloured pustules which start on the lower leaves and work up the plant). If you find it is present, then it is wise to consider a new mint bed each year. Examine your stock – if the roots show a large number of thickened new bud shoots (called bull shoots) discard them, and invest in new stock. When I bought my first three large sackfuls of mint roots I was delighted with the mint crop. Unfortunately, in my ignorance, I did not realize that one third of the roots were those of nettles! Although the mint was of excellent variety, I had a most uncomfortable time trying to cut it. It not only improved my knowledge of how to select good rootstock, but also taught me not to take for granted the knowledge of other growers!

Mulching and fertilizing

Mulch – a good squelchy sort of word, which covers a wide range of materials which fulfil several functions. A mulch can assist with weed control, conserve moisture, improve the soil, provide a path and unify and improve a garden. Some of the different types of mulches are listed below.

Black plastic

Held down by soil, bricks, etc this will give you good control and can last two seasons around established plants. Several widths, in long lengths, are available. It may be secured over a newly cultivated bed, holes cut and young plants inserted through and into the soil.

The disadvantages are that unless your ground is very level, pools of water may form and the surface become slippery; irrigation may miss some of the plant holes and the resident plants die from drought. Do put down slug bait before laying, and remember to position any watering tubes beneath the black plastic before securing the edges with soil – it can be very awkward to attempt to do it once the plants start to 'bush' out

Woven black polythene

This is more expensive but lasts much longer. It suppresses weed growth, while allowing air and natural rainfall to pass through. The narrow rolls make excellent paths and encourage worm (and slug) action. This material is very good as ground cover for a standing ground for pots in polytunnels which are in constant use.

Straw

Straw can be useful for larger plants. Unfortunately, it is very difficult to know whether modern cereal herbicides and pesticides have left any residues which may affect herb plants. So really this is best avoided, unless you are sure of the source and what chemicals the farmer has used over the cereal season.

Peat

Peat is a soil improver and an excellent mulch. It can, however, be difficult to prevent wind or water splash on the plants' lower leaves from any dust in the peat.

Bark

Bark is not cheap, but it makes light work of improving the appearance, retaining moisture in a dry season and suppressing weeds in a garden.

The large leaves of Angelica and Comfrey

These will gradually break down and improve soil texture if cast down between the rows, providing an organic mulch which the worms enjoy. Don't laugh – trees provide their own leaf mulch and benefit greatly from it!

Hoeing

By loosening the top tilth of the soil, you not only chop off seedling weeds, but also provide a natural aerated mulch and some healthy exercise for yourself. Cracked, hard soil dries out much faster than regularly hoed land. Even if it makes one smile to hear a gardening expert exhort us 'to keep that old hoe moving' it is very sound advice indeed.

Irrigation

Depending on your water source, and the pressure of the water, a little or a great deal of money may be expended on watering the crops. Good irrigation is essential for ensuring the germination of seedlings in dry conditions, and also to assist the plant to renew itself rapidly after cutting.

Watering methods – from simple to complex!

(a) Hand watering – always necessary somewhere!

(b) Lawn sprays – we used them for years.

(c) Perforated flat tubing – black plastic tubes with holes punched at intervals; very effective if you can secure it down without impeding the flow of water.

(d) Seepage hose, many types available.

(e) Drip irrigation; this requires a planned system of 'mains' and is very useful inside as well as along field crop rows.

(f) Overhead spraylines in houses.

(g) Standing spraylines with various sizes of spray heads for sales, stock and standing beds. These can be on spikes or stands.

(h) Portable spraylines – either 'fixed' sprays in long aluminium tubes on movable stands, or rotating sprays.

(i) Spray 'guns' – these can produce rather large heavy droplets for herb crops.

Eventually pressure boosters, filters, reduction valves etc are all required as the system becomes more sophisticated.

However simple the watering system may be, always remember the need for filtering any water source. Some may contain algae or even small fish that will block tubes and holes. It is infuriating and time-consuming to have to patiently clear out blocked holes etc with the aid of a darning needle stuck into a cork! Also the effect of sunlight on tubing can encourage a build-up of slime which needs to be flushed out before using the equipment.

If you are using lengths of hose, the wise use of matching brass connectors throughout the nursery will save much frustration and wasted time.

A supplier of irrigation equipment is given on page 156. After years of employing mixed systems and the increasing use of labour on watering we have had a total mixed system installed by experts – Prime Waterman have solved our problems, and it is absolute bliss to be able to turn a lever or press a button and know that water is available at the right time and being used in economical amounts wherever I need it on the nursery. The increased production and improvement in plants will soon, I hope, repay the capital cost.

Cutting

I generally do not call it 'harvesting' because that implies a once-only crop.

Whether you prefer scissors or knives, do make sure that they are clean and sharp. Not only is it tiring for the hand to use blunt tools, but mangling and damaging the plant may reduce the quantity of the next crop. Cleanliness is important to prevent transferring problems from one plant to another. Sticky blades retain and can pass on all kinds of germs or pests, so frequent soaking in a disinfectant solution is wise.

With feathery annuals like Dill, aim to cut above the growing point, so that regrowth will take place quickly. With bushier herbs, cut so as to train them into multiple-branched plants which will produce an abundance of leaves for the future. Never cut them back so hard that the plants have to struggle to renew themselves. The exceptions to these general rules would be plants which grow new shoots from the base, like Mint and Chives.

Cutting the crops should take place while it is still cool after the night, but any mist or dew should have dried from the foliage. Have to hand clean containers of standard size – your standard, so that you are able to form some idea of how many boxes, blue mushroom punnets (very useful for Chives), crates etc are required for the day's orders. Nothing is more frustrating, and time wasting, than having to rush off at the last minute to cut another half a box to fulfil an order. It is also galling to overcut a precious stock of some herb which is in rather short supply. Do try to be organized – have ready scissors or knives, a note of the quantity required, a list of varieties in hand, and be really business-like to start the day!

Once the herbs are cut, the containers must be placed in the shade until you have enough ready to take them to the packing area. If the herbs are exposed to the sun or wind they will soon look unhappy, and the volatile oils will be evaporating from the leaves. When the customer requires 'bunched' herbs like Mint,

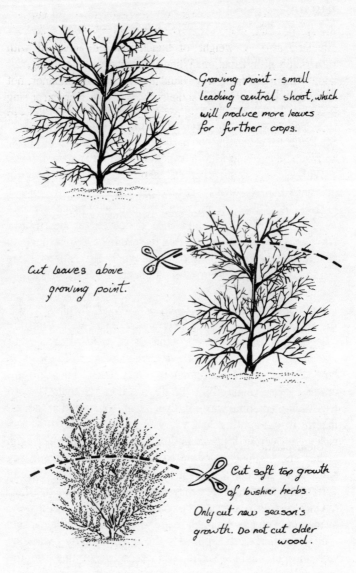

Growing point - small leading central shoot, which will produce more leaves for further crops.

Cut leaves above growing point.

Cut soft top growth of bushier herbs. Only cut new season's growth. Do not cut older wood.

Parsley or Chervil, then these are best bunched while cutting, the elastic bands being slipped on straightaway. With practice a standard size or weight of bunch can be achieved with remarkably little variation. When cutting herbs for packing, cut and lay them the same way round in rows, in the container, not in random handfuls. This sounds obvious, but it is surprising how many people have to be reminded how essential this is to speed the work of packing efficiently.

Packing

I have already emphasized the need for some form of packaging, not only for cleanliness, hygiene and the best possible shelf-life extent, but also for that indefinable something called 'presentation'. If you value the amount of care you have given to growing and cutting your herbs, and wish to make the best impression on your customer, then much thought should be given to the appearance of your herbs and how you want the world to see them. Perforated polythene bags, sometimes known as 'lettuce bags', are ideal for larger-sized, bunched types of herbs, eg Chervil, Coriander and Parsley.

Polystyrene trays overwrapped with cling or stretch film and heat-sealed beneath the trays, is an attractive method of presentation. These white or clear poly trays are very light, come in many sizes, and can be seen in most supermarkets. They are useful for softer herbs like Basil, Chives, Dill, Marjoram etc.

Clear plastic trays with or without lids are suitable for most herbs. They are manufactured in various depths, so can be used in a shallow size for Chives and French Tarragon, and the really deep type for Mint and Parsley. Local packaging suppliers may be found by studying the commercial section of the Telephone Directory – the Yellow Pages.

Labelling is essential for retail and supermarket sales. There are statutory regulations for the inclusion of 'sell by' dates, countries of origin, weights etc and these alter as each new

Iden Croft Herbs
Fresh Cut
THYME

ROSEMARY. Indispensable aromatic herb. Used traditionally with all roast meats, especially lamb and veal. Chicken pieces with rosemary, parsley & tarragon butter, apple jellies, jams & fruit salads.

FRENCH TARRAGON
FREEZE-DRIED
40 ml.
Reconstituted in seconds
IDEN CROFT HERBS

BASIL
USE IN SALADS, SAUCES, CHEESE AND PASTA. DELICIOUS WITH TOMATOES AND EGGS, ESSENTIAL IN ITALIAN COOKING. STRONG FLAVOUR. USE SPARINGLY AT FIRST.

Examples of labels for retailing fresh herbs. Each customer has set requirements about the 'sell by' date, usually 3 days. Weight should be on label if over 25g.

piece of legislation appears.* The British Herb Trade Association or National Farmers' Union are the people to consult if you need help. If you wish to encourage the buying public, then give some thought to the information often needed as to why one should buy a particular herb! Is it eaten raw, or cooked? If the latter, how? Why? When? With what? Having considered these points you can design your own labels, handouts and advertising material, imbuing it with your own personal touch. Don't just copy someone else's information – you may have a new and fresh reason for using that particular herb which hasn't occurred to everyone else. Use your love of herbs to put yourself into your customer's place and then give some clear and interesting information.

Herbs for wholesale supply are not usually individually labelled unless requested. The same details – type of herb, weight, etc – must appear on the outer box, also the name and address of the sender. Invent a simple logo if possible. It is simpler to see, and can be used on all your business invoices and letterheads. I tend to forget names – but a good logo impresses itself on my brain for life.

Standards

It is obvious that anything for edible use should be grown as clean, weed- and chemical-free as possible. Pests should not be nestling in the leaves, while old leaves and dead bits are totally banned. The whole flavour and aromatic property of the herb must be retained, otherwise it will alter or not give flavour when used. This means growing the plant so that the leaves and stems when cut are not 'woody', but also are not forced and too soft so that flavour is lacking. Luckily herbs are

---

*At the time of writing, all packages of herbs in excess of 25 grammes should have their weight displayed on the label. The exception to this is Saffron, which has to be so marked whatever the quantity being sold.

not too temperamental so normal good growing ensures all these qualities. Herbs in my view should not be sold bare in bunches. They soon wilt, and are open to dust, contamination, people's fingers (they can't resist squeezing the leaves!), and it must be admitted – theft. One pack or bag can be opened so that the herbs can be examined and enjoyed.

Continuity

This is simply explained. It is having enough herbs to cut daily, weekly or whenever, to supply your orders! Unfortunately, to be totally efficient in this, comes only with experience. The nearest horticultural equivalent would be intensive salad production. Only by trial and error, keeping records, experience and a dash of luck can this be successfully achieved, and no two growers in different areas would follow the same programme. Even the most experienced growers face shortages, therefore the main lesson to be learned from your records is why it happened. What can be done in the future to prevent a recurrence? Even then, all carefully laid plans can be wrecked by adverse weather so that – after an inexplicable gap in germination – everything grows at once. Now you will understand why farmers lean on gates gazing at their crops, deep in thought. Growers never seem to have a complete normal season. Each year is different, with new problems, or its unexpected triumphs over nature.

Average Growing and Harvesting
Months for Culinary Herbs. S.E. England

P = Protected * = Field Crops

	Jan	Feb	Mar	Apr	May	Jun	July	Aug	Sep	Oct	Nov	Dec
Angelica					*	*	*					
Basil			P	P	*	*	*	P*				
Borage			P	P*	*	*	*	*	*	P		
Chervil	P	P	P	*	*	*	*	*	*	*	P	P
Chives		P	P	P*	*	*	*	*	*	P*	P	P
Coriander			P*	*	*	*	*	*	*	*	P*	P
Dill				P	*	*	*	*	*	P*		
Fennel			P	P*	*	*	*	*	*	*	P*	
Lemon Balm			P	*	*	*	*	*	*	*	P	
Lovage			P*	*	*	*	*	*	*	*	P	
Marjoram (pot)			P	P*	*	*	*	*	*	P*	P	P
Marjoram (sweet)					P	*	*	*	*			
Mint (apple)				*	*	*	*	*	*	*	P*	
Mint (spear)	P	P	P	*	*	*	*	*	*	*	P*	P
Oregano			P	P*	*	*	*	*	*	*	P*	
Parsley	P	P	P	P	*	*	*	*	*	*	*	P
Rosemary	P	P	P	P*	*	*	*	*	*	*	P*	P
Sage	P	P	P	*	*	*	*	*	*	*	*	P*
Savory, (s)					P*	*	*	*	*	*		
Savory, (w)	P*	P*	*	*	*	*	*	*	*	*	P*	P*
Sorrel, large leaf			P	*	*	*	*	*	*	P		
Tarragon, French			P	P*	*	*	*	*	*	P*	P	
Thyme, culinary	P	P	P*	*	*	*	*	*	*	P*	P*	P*
Thyme, lemon	P	P	P*	*	*	*	*	*	*	P*	P*	P

(s) – Summer (w) – Winter

Seed Sowing and Propagation for Culinary Herbs. Approximate Months depending on Weather Conditions. S.E. England

Sch = Seed in cold house
SH = Seed in heated house – plant out later
S = Seed for field crops – direct drilled
D = Plant division
Pr = Propagation by cuttings

	Jan	Feb	Mar	Apr	May	Jun	July	Aug	Sep	Oct	Nov	Dec
Angelica							S	S	S			
Basil			SH	SH	SH S	S						
Borage		SH	SH	S	S	S	S					
Chervil		S	S	S	S	S	S		S	S		
Chives	D	D	D S	S	S	S				D	D	D
Coriander			S	S	S	S	S	S	S			
Dill		SH	S	S	S	S	S	S				
Fennel			SH	S	S	S						
Lemon Balm		D	D S	S	S					D	D	
Lovage			S	S			S	S		D	D	
Marjoram (pot)		D	D	Pr	Pr	Pr	Pr			D	D	
Marjoram (sweet)			S	S	S	S						
Mint(apple)	D	D	D Pr	Pr	Pr	Pr				D	D	D
Mint(spear)	D	D	D Pr	Pr	Pr	Pr				D	D	D
Oregano		D	D Pr	Pr	Pr	Pr				D	D	
Parsley	Sch	Sch	S	S	S		S	S	S	Sch	Sch	Sch
Rosemary			Pr	S Pr	S Pr	Pr	Pr	Pr	Pr	Pr		
Sage			S	S	Pr S	Pr	Pr			D	D	
Savory(s)			S	S	S	S						
Savory(w)			Pr	Pr	Pr	Pr		S	S	Pr	Pr	
Sorrel, large-leaf	D	D S	S	S						D	D	
Tarragon, French	D	D Pr	Pr	Pr	Pr					D	D	
Thyme, culinary	Pr/	DSP/DSPr/	S Pr	Pr	Pr	Pr	Pr	Pr	Pr	Pr		
Thyme, lemon	Pr/	D P/	D Pr/	Pr	Pr	Pr	Pr	Pr	Pr	Pr		

(s) – Summer (w) – Winter

6

Drying, freezing and freeze~drying herbs

Books written about herbs usually contain a small section on the art of drying herbs, which is beautifully illustrated with old woodcuts showing monks at work with pestle and mortar, large bunches of herbs hanging from beams in the background – a scene of tranquillity and learning. Even more delightful are the pictures of the good housewife at work in her stillroom, teaching the younger members of the household the mysteries of drying and blending herbs into the various preparations required for the daily health and use of a large household. Little reference is usually made to the skill, time, and equipment required if you wish to produce more than a domestic supply of dried herbs yourself. The old herbals and stillroom recipes are a joy to read and adapt, but tend not to mention the number of helpers who were involved, either unpaid or at very low wages, and the knowledge and skill essential for preserving the virtues of herbs for winter.

Drying herbs

The aim of drying is to preserve the natural oils of the herb, which are known as 'essential' oils. This enables one to use the flavour and properties of the plant at all seasons of the year. It is ironical that the culinary herbs which dry most successfully, are also available in the garden in winter, ie Bay, Rosemary, Savory and Thyme. The softer but strong-flavoured Chervil, Dill, Fennel, Parsley and Sage require more care, but can remain green and full of flavour when dried. A cold and wet growing season may produce a change in quality of the aromatic oil content of herbs, which in turn can alter the final results however good the drying technique.

Although most people think immediately of culinary herbs when drying is mentioned, do not forget the aromatic, medicinal and cosmetic uses of the plants. If you only have small-scale facilities, it would be pointless to compete with the present large-scale production of the common culinary herbs. Small quantities of special herbs grown to order for a medicinal herbalist, or a range of aromatic leaves and flowers for direct sale to the public, may be grown on a spare acre or so of land. A well-planned, large garden will produce an astonishing amount of flowers and leaf material, and this, with a few purchased 'extras', can make personal pot-pourri blends that are quite unique. Whatever you decide to do, the following general rules are important:

Cutting

Do make sure you are growing and cutting the correct herb! I have known people mistake Scentless Mayweed, Corn Chamomile (*Anthemis matricaria inodora*), for German Chamomile (*Matricaria recutita*). Another important point is that not all herbs will retain their strength and typical aroma when dried; it mysteriously disappears! Dry a trial batch first before embarking on a large-scale planting programme for drying, and check with a herb specialist if you are in any doubt.

It is wise to cut only the quantity of material that can be dealt with *on one day*. If kept cut and undried the plants will quickly deteriorate. Separate each batch and label – don't be tempted to mix several together.

The moisture content of most plants is well above 70 per cent so a considerable quantity of fresh material is required to produce the dried result. One should obtain roughly 1 lb (0.5 kg) of dried herb from every 8–9 lb (3·5–4 kg) of fresh material. Choose a day with good dry weather and a low humidity level, and do not water the plants during the previous two days. Wet weather can be a great problem and you will have to become an amateur weather forecaster! Cut the herbs early in the day once the dew has evaporated and the plants are dry. It is important that contamination from animals, petrol or diesel fumes should be avoided, or from any chemical crop sprays that may have drifted from a neighbouring field. The time of cutting will also vary according to the part or parts of the plant required. Generally it is usual to take the plant when the oil or medicinal ingredient is at its strongest. There is little point in collecting roots when the plant is abundant with leaves and flowers, because the root will probably be at its best when autumn slows down growth and it will be plump and full of the active principle required. If the entire plant is required, usually it should be in full bloom, and the root must be washed clean.

Plants with soft growth which dies down in the winter may be cut almost to ground level; they will then provide a second or third flush of growth for drying. Such plants include Marjorams, Melissa, Mints, Oregano etc.

Plants which have woody stems are best cut back to the previous year's growth level – unless they are newly planted. These include Rosemary, Sage, Savory (winter), Thyme.

Leaves are at their best for drying purposes if taken before the flowers open. Flowers vary; some are best dried when half open, others just fully open, so that all possible essential oil is retained. Be careful to avoid damaging flowers by too much handling; try to cut or shake onto the drying tray as soon as possible.

Collect the herb material into flat collecting boxes or trays; deterioration can be rapid if they are heaped up. Drying should be started as soon as possible after picking and should be a continuous process. If left 'damp' for a short time a musty smell soon develops and the herb product is spoilt.

Where to dry

I have seen so many bright ideas for drying on a fairly small scale, that I feel it is best left to you to assess your own possible areas and to use DIY methods ingeniously. The main requirements are warmth, ventilation, shade, and racks for the herbs. Do not dry herbs in bunches (unless a *bouquet garni* mixture is required, which would be too brittle if put together when dry). The centre of the bunch usually tends to be less dry than the outer leaves, which can lead to mustiness and strange flavours. Conversely, if the centre of the bunch is dry, the outer leaves may become too brittle and crumble to dust. Bunches hanging over the kitchen stove may look picturesque, but in the rising warm air there will be dust, grease, and cooking smells – not too hygienic! It may seem a more speedy method to bunch herbs together and hang in a drying cupboard, but this can be more time-consuming in the end because you have to carefully check that they are properly dried.

Many people start by using a large airing cupboard. This can be satisfactory providing the ventilation is good. Ideally, the dry air should enter at the bottom, and the warm damp air escape at the top. Racks may be made to fit on to batons, which are fixed on the side walls, the number of racks being limited only by the size of the cupboard.

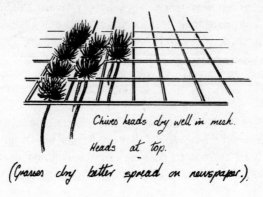

Chives heads dry well in mesh.
Heads at top.
(Grasses dry better spread on newspaper.)

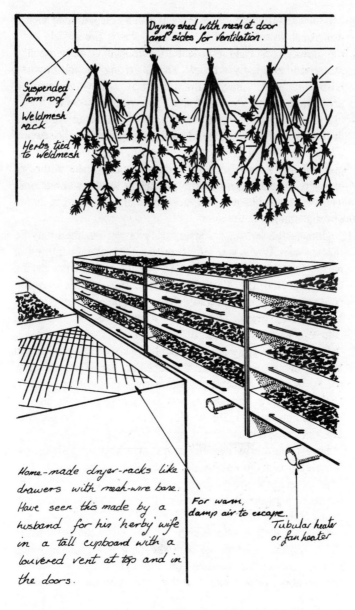

Drying shed with mesh at door and sides for ventilation.

Suspended from roof

Weldmesh rack

Herbs tied to weldmesh

Home-made dryer-racks like drawers with mesh-wire base. Have seen this made by a husband for his 'herby' wife in a tall cupboard with a louvered vent at top and in the doors.

For warm, damp air to escape.

Tubular heater or fan heater

A drying area may be constructed in an alcove or against a wall using dowelling rods. Very light plastic tubes slide over the dowel rods, and cotton butter muslin is attached and stretched between the tubes. This is strong enough because herbs are light. Leaving the top 'rack' empty can provide protection against dust and allow free passage of air.

A well-ventilated room or airy attic can be utilized as a drying room. However, avoid strong sunlight. If you are drying a large quantity of herbs at one time a heater (which does not give off any fumes) may be required – especially if the air humidity is high owing to the prevailing weather conditions. Tubular electric heaters are used by many people, fan 'blowers' by others.

Outside the house, a conservatory or garden shed may be the answer. When you get to producing larger quantities of herbs, it will be more difficult to provide the correct drying conditions and the time has then come to research the commercial drying machinery. This will mean greater capital expenditure, larger output, better quality control – and of course a well-researched selling outlet!

Racks for drying herbs should be covered with cotton muslin, or strong hessian if the racks are large. Never allow the herbs to come in contact with wire or metal. Being able to slide the racks in and out easily when turning and checking the herbs is important. Light wooden frames with corner pieces to prevent distortion are fairly simple to make.

Spread the herbs evenly on the racks and try to keep the temperature at approximately 90°F. (30°C.) for twenty-four hours, turning the herbs over several times. This reduces the moisture content of the material rapidly while retaining the main, active ingredient.

After the first twenty-four hours lower the temperature to 75°F. (25°C.) – 80°F. (27°C.), keeping the process even, without cooking or overheating. The drying herbs will need turning about once a day, and the rack to be turned around –

this will ensure even drying. If fresh material has to be taken into the drying room, place it on the top shelves so that the ventilation will remove the moisture given off by the newly cut herbs.

Herbs vary in the time required to dry, anything from four to seven days depending on the type of leaf and stem.

How can you tell when the herbs are ready?

Flower petals will feel dry and 'papery'. With leaf and stem herbs, the stem should snap easily. Fully dried leaves will part from the stems and this can be tested by rubbing the sprig gently between the palms of the hands. Roots should be dry right through and break easily with no 'corky' core inside. Seeds should 'crack' and crumble between finger nails. Leaves should be brittle and aromatic, not brown and 'overdone', and should crumble, but not into dust! Experience will teach you more than can be described in words. A simple test for dryness would be to place some herbs in a tightly lidded, dry glass jar and leave them in a warm place for several hours. If there is the slightest sign of condensation on the glass, the drying process is not complete.

Finishing and rubbing down

If you are 'finishing' a fairly large quantity of dried herbs, do use thin cotton gloves and wear a dust mask. Small quantities of leaves may be rubbed off the stalks between the fingers onto clean paper. Pick out and discard all bits of dried stick, badly coloured herbs etc and then rub the herbs methodically between the palms of the hands over a clean box. Most medicinal and cosmetic uses do not require too small a herb – find out what the particular customer requires.

Storage

Essential oils are destroyed by light, heat, moisture and time – so store your dried herbs in well-labelled, dated, air-tight containers. Guard against mice, beetles, moths, insects – they all love the pleasantly aromatic herbs!

Your stock of dried herbs will gradually deteriorate. When the next drying season comes round, use the dry, unsaleable old stock to sprinkle round the plants in your garden – it will be most beneficial as a good, organic material and certain herbs – Feverfew, Tansy, Rue, Pennyroyal, will also act as useful insect repellants.

Drying aromatic leaves for use in the home and for gift items

All the general rules for drying apply whether you are going to produce a small quantity for making gift sachets or drying tonnes for an industry. The large producer will have been contracted to produce for a dryer or wholesaler, and will probably be producing a single herb product – eg Sage or Thyme.

The skill of blending dried herbs and flowers for aromatic use depends on your feeling for harmony and balance in your sense of smell – in other words, your 'nose'. Very few people have the 'nose' to detect the subtle differences and possible blends in the basic ingredients which go to make a new and exciting fragrance that will last, and not alter with keeping. Many of us can develop a talent for detecting when a finished blend is 'right'. It is wise to use a tried and tested recipe for mixing pot-pourri and aromatic oils, and then using small quantities at a time test the effect of adding measured amounts of further ingredients. This sounds rather like a cookery recipe – and in a way the same rules apply; a heavy hand with an extra ingredient thrown in for good measure can ruin a cake, or produce a pot-pourri blend that smells like a strong lavatory cleaner.

There are some excellent books available on aromatics, and all the myriads of things one can do with them. If this is your particular interest, see page 153.

One factor I feel to be most important – entirely natural materials should be used if possible. The cost of a natural 'essential' oil of good quality, to put in your pot-pourri mixture, will be considerably higher than the artificial equivalent, although I must admit that in some cases the difference is hardly discernible. However, in the finished product, too great a use of cheaper oils can produce a 'sameness' of smell which hardly alters whether the pot-pourri is warm or cool, kept lidded or open to the air. To me the whole elusive charm of pot-pourri is then lost, because I love the way a natural blend alters gently with warmth, and mellows with time. In the home one can re-awaken and strengthen an old pot-pourri with a few added ingredients stirred in with a few drops of alcohol. (I use vodka – it is almost 100 per cent pure.) Larger quantities of pot-pourri can be stored successfully for some time in damp-proof containers. They should *never* be stored in sacks in a damp place, since musty pot-pourri cannot be restored. Also, beware of mice and insects.

I am always fascinated by the effects of aromatics on mood and health – greater, I think, than we all realize. Two of the most popular blends with the general public would seem to be Rose, and anything with a fresh citrus smell – for example, Lemon Verbena. If you are unable to grow and dry sufficient quantities for your needs, or require extra ingredients and spices in bulk, a list of useful wholesale suppliers is given on page 155.

Herbal gifts

Attractively made sachets, pillows, posies, garlands for festive occasions are all popular; they attract people wishing to give a personal gift to any age of relative or friend. Men seem to like herbal gifts, so don't forget to design some with them in mind. Anyone with a talent for making or designing these items will find it helpful to visit trade gift fairs, public exhibitions, and shops specializing in similar products. I often feel it is true that there is nothing really new, but the clever adaptation of an idea, the use of different materials or unusual shapes can make all the difference to the sales appeal of a quite ordinary item. If

Ideas for
Gift Packaging.

possible pack your finished product into something shiny that enhances it, feels nice; add an attractive label explaining its use, the reason for making it. All these touches show care!

Herbs with aromatic leaves and flowers

Alecost	(*Chrysanthemum balsamita tanacetoides* syn. *Balsamita major tanacetoides*)
Angelica	(*Angelica archangelica*)
Artemisias	
Balm of Gilead	(*Cedronella triphylla*) (Not *populus gileadensis*, but very aromatic)
Basil	(*Ocimum basilicum*)
Bay	(*Laurus nobilis*)
Bergamot	(*Monarda didyma*)
Calamint	(*Calamintha grandiflora*)
Camphor plant	(*Balsamita vulgaris*)
Chamomile	(*Anthemis nobile*)
Cotton Lavender	(*Santolina chamaecyparissus* and other varieties)
Curry plant	(*Helichrysum angustifolium*)
Eucalyptus, lemon	(*Eucalyptus citriodora*)
Hops	(*Humulus lupulus*)
Hyssop	(*Hyssopus officinalis*)
Lavenders	(*Lavandula*, many varieties)
Lemon Balm	(*Melissa officinalis*)
Lovage	(*Levisticum officinale*)
Marjoram, wild	(*Origanum vulgare*)
Marjoram, sweet	(*Origanum majorana*)
Meadowsweet	(*Filipendula ulmaria*)
Melilot	(*Melilotus officinalis*)
Mint	(*Mentha*, many varieties)
Myrtle	(*Myrtus communis*)
Pelargoniums	Aromatic-leaf varieties
Pinks	(*Dianthus*, clove-scented varieties)

Roses	(*Rosa*, sweet-smelling varieties)
Rosemary	(*Rosmarinus officinalis*)
Sage	(*Salvia officinalis*)
Sage, pineapple	(*Salvia rutilans*)
Southernwood	(*Artemisia abrotanum*)
Thymes	(*Thymus*, many varieties and fragrances)
Verbena, lemon	(*Lippia citriodora*)
Woodruff, sweet	(*Asperula odorata* syn. *gallium odoratum*)

Frozen and freeze-dried herbs

These are used mainly in the catering industry, but are also extremely useful for domestic use, delicatessens, and specialist producers of a seasonal dish – for example, Dill for gravad lax (pickled) salmon. Frozen herbs are particularly useful when incorporated within a dish while freeze-dried herbs can be accurately measured for portion control when scattered on the prepared packs. Examples of these recipe dishes may be seen in any well-stocked supermarket chill cabinet, and it is obvious that good colour and flavour are essential.

Frozen herbs

There is a world of difference between freezing herbs for one's own use in the domestic freezer, and producing fresh herbs in bulk for the freezing industry. Some herbs, ie Basil, do not dry really successfully but a great deal of the colour and flavour will be retained when put through specialist freezing processors. Most people who have experimented for their own use will have discovered that freshly cut, washed, and quickly frozen Chervil, Coriander, Dill, Parsley etc are extremely useful in winter when supplies are limited. The preparation of frozen herbs for the catering industry requires expensive investment in machinery to wash, dry, chop and quick freeze the herbs into a crumb form, then store the finished product in bulk at the correct temperature. Transport has to be at the correct temperature also. Many food regulations, standards, and bacterial checks have to be taken into consideration in production and it is obvious that a large tonnage has to be processed at one time to make the whole operation cost effective.

The processor usually contracts with growers and farmers to grow the crops so they reach maturity at times which will ensure continuous use of the machinery and supply continuous orders. I do not therefore feel it is a wise choice of growing for anyone without experience on less than 10 acres (4ha) of land. However if you have land and growing experience and live near to a processing firm, it will do no harm to find out if they are interested in finding new growers for a particular crop.

Freeze drying

This process is a bit mysterious to me, and seems a well-kept secret by the successful producers. It is an expensive process, but produces a well-flavoured light dry herb of good colour. The fresh herbs used must be of top quality and at the peak of condition to be acceptable for processing. In simple layman terms I understand them to be 'free flow frozen', all the moisture being removed in a vacuum so rapidly that the herb has no time to deteriorate and lose its essential oil. The end result is what really matters, and the herbs certainly rehydrate rapidly and produce an acceptable alternative to the best flavoured product (fresh!).

Approximately 20lb (9kg) of fresh herbs will yield 2.2lb (1kg) of freeze-dried product, which will rehydrate to about 17.5lb (8kg). Again, not an advisable project for anyone with a small acreage and insufficient growing experience.

With both frozen and freeze-dried herbs the time between cutting and delivery to the processor must be as brief as possible, and this is usually stipulated in the growing contract.

7
Creating a herb garden

This, for me, is the most enjoyable facet of being a herb grower, and is important if you are planning to deal directly with the public and there is sufficient space to demonstrate your abilities with plants. Unfortunately, when creating a garden it is never perfect, but you know that there is always 'next year'! When it is your own private garden, you will see and appreciate the changes as the year progresses, and your mind's eye will impose upon the reality the effect you are trying to create.

When you plant and develop a public garden, remember that it will be seen by individuals, who will retain the memory of your garden as it was on the particular day of the year on which they visited. Careful planning and maintenance will be necessary to present a changing but always attractive picture.

Delightful gardens can just happen accidentally, but normally a great deal of thought and a clear objective make for the most successful and natural results. Your garden will be sterile unless it has some individual imprint and originality, otherwise why should it be there at all?

Planning
I find it helps to measure carefully and plan on graph paper,

even if I don't adhere strictly to the plan later. The area should be one that will be manageable when weeding and trimming become necessary. Don't be carried away by enthusiasm and find you cannot keep up with general maintenance – a mulch will help to suppress the weeds, but there will always be some work to be done.

Once the permanent features are on your graph paper, the next point to consider is how are the public to see your garden. Where are you to site the paths? If the garden is small, then the paths must be around its borders but make them at least wide enough for two people to walk together or to comfortably pass each other. Single-file traffic is frustrating, and usually results in heavy footprints in the beds or borders. If your general access is good and the site level, make allowance for the width of wheelchairs, so that the disabled have the freedom to enjoy your garden too. Unless the garden is to be of a formal type in straight lines and regular beds, you have the opportunity to create surprise vistas by allowing the paths to bend and curve. No one really likes retracing their footsteps, so it is better if the paths can always be leading somewhere, even if it is only to the way out and, most important, past the sales area! To enter and exit at the same point may lead to a traffic jam of visitors which will destroy the peaceful image of your herb garden.

The paths may be of gravel, brick or pavings. Bark mulch is attractive – and drains quickly to produce a dry surface. Seats are important (if there is sufficient space). It is a compliment to you if someone feels it worth while to sit and admire your masterpiece for a long time, providing they haven't been overcome by all the fragrant delights and fallen asleep! If the site seems too level and uninteresting, take this opportunity to sink paths and terraces, make slopes and banks. Size is not as important as most people seem to think. Scotney Castle in Kent has a delightfully small garden; Hatfield House a magnificently large one – but both give equal pleasure. It is worth

Example of a small town front garden. The owner knew exactly what she wanted to use - it was a question of how to fit it all in!

Existing hedge

while taking time to look at some of the many herb gardens in Great Britain or America to analyse what you like (or dislike) about them. Although there is nothing new, you will begin to form your own ideas of how you feel herbs should be displayed. If time and finance limit chances to see for yourself, there are books now available with superb photographs of well known and fairly unknown herb gardens all over the world.

Look at the site carefully; does it contain any desirable features that you can incorporate into the general design? A beautiful tree, a pool of water, a sloping bank or a stream? Do you need to hide any unpleasant buildings, or a view of the local bus station? Perhaps you are fortunate in possessing a distant view of the countryside that may be featured, framed in herbs and roses. Plan a seat where the view can be best seen and enjoyed.

Soil and aspect must be considered. If the site is windswept and facing north, obviously sheltering hedges or walls are

1 Rosemary (officinalis and prostrate)
2 Rosemary (Fota Blue)
3 Lavenders
4 Dill
5 Anise Hyssop
6 Thyme 'Silver Posie'
7 Sage
8 { Red Sage,
    Pineapple Mint,
    Golden Sage
9 Bay Tree,
  various Thymes,
  Lavender 'Munstead Dwarf'
  and Chives.

10 { Ladies Mantle
     Giant Chives
     Welsh Onion
     Black Peppermint
11 { Pot Marjoram
     Lemon Verbena
     French Sorrel
     Winter Savory
     Summer Savory
     Rock Hyssop
     Compact Marjoram
     Oregano
     Garlic Chives
     Chamomile

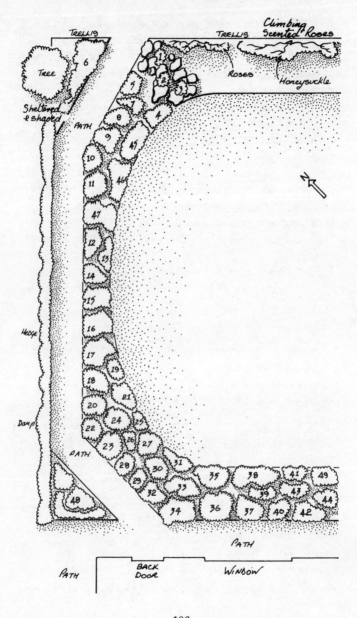

Example of an informal herb garden. Based on an actual garden. The aim was to create a useable but decorative border, planting in groups of 3 or 5 to provide quick cover and a mature appearance.

1 Creeping Pennyroyal
2 'Treneague' Chamomile
3 Wild Thyme (drucei minus) } to smell nice between path and stones
4 Thyme 'Archus Gold' for brighter edge
5 Cotton Lavender
⑥ Myrtle
7 Rosemary (officinalis)
8 Lavender 'Seale'
9 Angelica
10 Lovage
11 Soapwort
12 Rue
13 Lemon Balm, variegated
⑭ Red Fennel
15 Green Fennel
16 Bergamot
17 Oregano
18 Curry Plant
19 Golden tipped Marjoram
20 French, large-leaved Sorrel
21 Dwarf Curry Plant
22 Purple Sage
23 Broad-leaved Sage
24 Golden Sage
25 'Doone Valley' creeping lemon Thyme
26 Mace
27 Compact Marjoram
28 Parsley
29 Garlic Chives

30 Pot Marjoram
31 Wild creeping Thyme (pulegioides)
32 Chives
㉝ French Tarragon
34 Rock Hyssop
35 Thyme 'Silver Posie
36 Lemon Thyme
37 Winter Savory
38 Chamomile, double-flowered
39 Chervil (sow seed in autumn and early spring)
40 Southernwood
41 Houseleeks
42 Upright Pennyroyal
㊸ Dill
㊹ Coriander (sow seeds)
㊺ Red Basil
㊻ Sweet Basil
㊼ Lemon Bergamot
48 Mints: apple, spearmint and peppermint
49 Golden lemon Thyme

Ringed numbers for planting in Spring, rest in Autumn

essential. To enter a sheltered aromatic garden when the wind is buffeting the walls or hedges outside is like being transported into a new (and better) world.

Prepare the site by digging or cultivating in plenty of compost to produce an open well-drained and aerated soil, removing all perennial weeds. Rich fertilizers or farmyard manure are unnecessary unless your soil is very deficient in nitrogen. If the area is large, or has been cropped intensively, it is wise to have a soil test analysis and seek advice on how to rectify any deficiencies.

Your canvas is now in front of you; how will you paint the picture? The most usual idea and an effective way to promote the sale of plants is a demonstration garden, simply showing how plants will look when mature in height and flowering habits. It is very difficult for customers, who need advice if they are just starting their first herb garden, to visualize the eventual beauty of a plant. A dear little Lovage or Angelica in a pot does not look like the dramatic plant it will become. Excellent in the right place, but ridiculous in a tiny patch 'by the back door'.

Clear, easy-to-read labels are essential if your garden is to fulfil its role, and it helps to have groups of plants with similar uses – culinary, medicinal etc. The customer with a particular interest can then see how the various plants will look against one another. If possible, the garden should be sited near to the sales area for pot plants. People don't like trotting backwards and forwards trying to remember names, and you will be missing a sales opportunity.

If you have particular interests and sufficient space, a theme garden is fascinating to visitors: culinary, medieval and aromatic themes are always interesting and educational. What about considering some of the following suggestions – further research is up to you. Collecting certain kinds of herb plants is one of the most addictive hobbies ever!

Silver and white
Foliage plants
Artemisias: Wormwood, Southernwood, Schmidtiana,
  Lanata pedamonta
Cotton Lavenders, Curry Plant
Lambs' Ears (*Stachys lanata*), Lavender
Mint, variegated apple; Mullein
Sage, Sea Holly
Thyme (*Lanuginosus* and *Alba*)

White flowers or seeds
Caraway, Chervil, Garlic Chives, Coriander
Honesty
Lily of the Valley
Meadowsweet, Melilot (White)
Onion, Welsh
Peony (White)
Roses (White)
Solomon's Seal, Sweet Cicely
Violets (White)
Woodruff

Elizabethan or Shakespearean Garden
Adonis
Bay, Borage, Box, Broom
Caraway, Carnation, Clover, Columbine, Cotton Lavender,
  Cowslip, Cuckoo flowers (Ranunculus)
Daffodil, Daisy, Delphinium
Elder
Fennel, Fumitory
Garlic
Harebell, Hawthorn, Holy Thistle, Holly, Hyssop
Iris, Ivy
Lily, Lady's Smock, Lavender, Larks' heels (Delphinium)

Marigold, Marjoram, Melissa, Mint, Mistletoe, Musk Rose,
   Mustard, Myrtle
Narcissus, Nasturtium
Ox-eye Daisy, Oxlip
Pansy, Parsley, Peony, Pinks, Plantain, Poppies, Primrose,
   Purslane
Rocket, Rosemary, Rue
Saffron Crocus, Savory (winter), Sorrel, Strawberry,
   Sunflower, Sweet Briar
Thyme, Wild Thyme
Violets
Woodbine, Wormwood
Yarrow, Yew

The witches' herbs are interesting if included in this garden –
but do label clearly the poisonous plants! Aconitum, Hemlock,

Hemlock

Opium Poppy

Henbane and Opium Poppy are poisonous. Fern and Mandrake are interesting, but should be planted well out of reach of tiny fingers.

I'm sure I have missed some, but I'll leave you to look up the quotations!

Dyer's garden

Natural dyes are becoming popular again. If you can erect information boards depicting the colours that plants will produce, and the mordant required, your garden could be of interest to schools and women's groups, as well as the natural-dye enthusiasts.

Birch, Black Alder, Blackberry, Blackthorn, Black Walnut,
    Bloodroot, Broom (Dyer's or Greenweed)
Carrot, Chamomile (Dyer's), Cleavers, Coltsfoot,
Dandelion

Elder, Elecampane
Fumitory
Golden Rod
Heathers, Hollyhock, Hops
Juniper (berries)
Lady's Bedstraw, Lady's Mantle
Madder, Marigold, Meadowsweet, Motherwort
Nettle
Onion
Pokeroot (berries), Privet
Safflower (flowers), St John's Wort, Sorrel, Sumac
Tansy
Weld, (Dyer's)
Woad
Woodruff (Dyer's)

Tea garden
To illustrate the beauty and uses of herbs for tisanes and refreshing drinks. I always feel this should be a garden where one can sit and sip!
Alecost, Angelica
Basil, Bergamot, Blackberry, Blackcurrant, Borage
Catnip, Chamomile, Clover
Dandelion
Elderflower
Fennel
Hops, Horehound, Hyssop
Lavender, Lemon Balm (Melissa), Lemon Thyme, Lime
    flowers, Liquorice, Lovage
Marigold, Marjoram, Mint
Parsley, Peppermint
Rose, Rosehip, Rosemary
Sage, Salad Burnet, Sweet Cicely
Thyme
Verbena (Lemon)

Violet (Sweet)
Woodruff
Yarrow

Bee and butterfly garden

One of my favourites. Single-flowered cultivars are more useful to bees.

For Bees

Aconite (winter), Alkanet, Anise

Basil, Bear's Breeches, Bergamot, Borage

Catmint, Catnip, Celandine, Chamomile (Dyer's), Chicory,
  Chives, Clematis, Clover (red or white), Coltsfoot,
  Comfrey, Cornflower, Cranesbill

Evening Primrose

Feverfew, Fennel, Field Scabious, Figwort, Fleabane

Gayfeather, Globe Thistle, Golden Rod

Heliotrope (winter), Hemp Agrimony, Hollyhock, Honesty,
  Honeysuckle, Horehound, Hyssop

Jacob's Ladder

Lambs' Ears. Lavender, Lily of the Valley, Lungwort

Mallow, Marigold, Marjorams, Marsh Marigold, Meadow
  Saffron, Meadowsweet, Melilot, Mignonette,
  Motherwort, Mullein

Origanum Dictamnus albus

Passionflower, Peony, Poppy, Purple Loosestrife,
  Pyrethrum

Sage, Savory, Sea Holly, Sea Lavender, Snowdrop,
  Solomon's Seal, Stonecrop, Sunflower, Sweet William

Tansy, Teazle, Thrift, Thymes, Toadflax

Vervain, Viper's Bugloss

Wallflower, Woad, Wood Sage

Yarrow, Yellow Loosestrife

Small trees valuable to bees include Crap Apples, Maple, Ornamental Cherry (*Prunus*). Shrubs enjoyed by bees include

Berberis (most varieties), Bladdersenna, Broom, Buddleia, Cotoneaster, Genista (for bumble bees), Mahonia, Privet, Willows.

For butterflies
Butterfly nectar plants
Bugle

Catmint, Coltsfoot, Corncockle, Cornflower, Cowslip

Dianthus

Echinops, Echium

Fenugreek

Goldenrod

Harebell, Heartsease, Helenium, Helianthemum, Honesty, Honeysuckle, Hyssop

Knapweed (Greater)

Lady's Bedstraw, Lady's Smock, Larkspur, Lavender, Lupin (tree)

Mallow, Marjoram (pot), Mignonette, Milk Thistle, Monkshood

Nicotiana

Ox-eye Daisy

Primrose, Prunella, Purple Loosestrife, Purple Toadflax

Ragged Robin, Rosemary

Scottish Thistle, Sedum, Soapwort, Sweet Rocket, St John's Wort

Thrift, Thymes

Valerian (red)

Vetch, Kidney

Yarrow

Butterfly larval plants
Cowslip

Fennel, Foxglove

Greenweed (Dyer's)

Heartsease, Honeysuckle, Horseradish

Lady's Bedstraw, Lady's Smock

Marshmallow, Mignonette, Musk Mallow

Pea, (Everlasting) Primrose
Rocket (Sweet)
Vetch (Kidney), Violet (Sweet)
Wild Strawberry

Other themes could be based on Roman gardens, herbs of the Bible, pot-pourri, astrology, Victorian posies, herbs for flower arrangers, knot gardens, cosmetic herbs, love gardens and many more! If you have difficulty in obtaining plants a list of herb farms and nurseries is given on page 155.

Records

Unless your memory has total recall the keeping of records is vital. I have a friend who is a real plantswoman. She knows the name of each plant in her superb garden, and can even tell you the nursery where it was purchased and the cost. The secret of her marvellous memory is her planting records, kept in school exercise books going back thirty-two years! This is an invaluable method if one wishes to renew a planting, or moves house and has to leave one's favourite plants behind. My records are not so accurate, but I do take endless photographs at different times of the year to establish when the various flowering seasons are, and for winter planning.

Herb gardens can look 'mature' quite rapidly if plants are grouped in threes or fives to give the effect of a year's growth.

Garden visitors and customers

After considering these ideas for beautiful gardens, it does seem a little mundane to think about the basic necessities for the visitors to your garden. After a long drive, often the first question asked is 'Do you have a toilet?' If you can provide even one toilet, put up a discreet but clear sign in the car park. Organize parking spaces well, so drivers can park with ease; it is surprising how many cannot reverse!

The next question may well be 'Is it possible to have a cup of tea?', or coffee, soft drink etc. Refreshments can be simple or elaborate, it depends on the number of visitors and your facilities. Most visitors are grateful for tea or coffee, with Coke or fruit squash for the younger ones. Crisps and biscuits all help to prevent hunger forcing people to leave earlier than intended.

Insurance

Check your situation regarding public liability insurance if you are going to have visitors to your garden, or retail customers calling for plants. Any good insurance firm will advise on this.

National collections

During the past few years an excellent scheme has come into being, instigated by the Royal Horticultural Society and based at Wisley. Many collections of plant species have been assigned to large and small nurseries all over Great Britain. In time these will be able to help with identification problems.

My own collection is of origanums, which has proved more difficult than I realized! Although it is a long way from completion, I have found many useful and beautiful varieties under different names. The true origanum, *onites* (pot Marjoram), is particularly striking and a marvellous plant for butterflies.

The address of the National Council for the Conservation of Plants and Gardens is given on page 151. The voluntary work done by its members is proving immensely valuable in finding and identifying plants that were becoming rare and difficult to obtain from modern nurseries.

8

Selling your herbs

Once you have decided to take the plunge and sell your herbs, it doesn't matter whether it is to your friends at the local fund-raising day, or a national campaign to convince everyone to eat more of your fresh herbs. Stop and think about the people who will be most important to your enterprise – your prospective customers.

What do you know about them? Start with yourself – you are someone's customer nearly every day; look carefully at what you buy and why? Analyse (if possible) what made you choose one washing powder rather than another, one type of magazine from the other twenty on view. Select an item that was really an 'impulse' buy, not on your list that day. Try to think why, and list the reasons it caught your eye, why it gives you pleasure, why you actually paid good money for it! Sometimes the answers come easily; very often we are unaware of the experiences and attitudes from childhood onwards that subconsciously influence our choice.

Spend some time observing the buying habits of others. Although we are all unique, we do tend to fall into 'groups' by age, family backgrounds, extrovert or introvert interests and occupations. This is the whole basis of market research. It is easier when embarking on a new venture if you are producing something which will appeal to a group in which you yourself feel at ease. If you have a flair for producing something new and unusual, and you believe in it, then you should be able to sell it, providing the group is not too small and eccentric – say Trappist monks!

Packaging and presentation

Once you have identified the group of customers you wish to attract, then your aim will be to make a good product look as attractive as possible, at a tempting price, without too much extra cost to yourself! Herb plants in pleasing pots and well labelled, almost sell themselves. Look carefully around any good garden centre – one can learn a great deal here about presentation and positioning of plants for maximum sales. Think how many plants are bought on impulse, simply because they are in flower and in a position near the till to catch the eye as the customer is leaving. White trays to contrast with foliage, plastic pot-sleeves to protect the plant until it reaches its new home, groups of herbs in suitable terra-cotta pots or hanging baskets – these all reinforce the message that herbs are useful and beautiful everywhere.

Presentation of fresh cut herbs is equally important – as discussed in Chapter 5. Dried culinary herbs need clear labels and ideas for using them. With aromatic dried herbs, you can be as imaginative as you wish. A large basket of beautiful pot-pourri scenting the air, with a notice inviting people to stir it with their hands, is a simple method of presentation. Remember to leave bags and measures beside the bowl otherwise your efforts will be wasted.

Don't get despondent if one of your best efforts doesn't sell. It sometimes needs several slight changes in presentation before success is achieved. You can't make people buy it if they don't want to. You simply have to go back to square one and try a different approach.

Indirect selling

When an agent, salesman, or garden centre is selling your herbs, do take an interest in what happens to your products. It will help to sell more if the agent knows you are interested in his customer's reactions and comments. Once you establish a good relationship with a wholesale outlet, you will get

Herb plants sell well if planted in terra-cotta pots.

forewarned of dips and heights in the demand, and advised where to increase your range of plants. Listening to people is as important as talking to them.

How to let the public know you are there!

With the proviso that you have a good product, full knowledge of it, and enough to sell, you must always let people know you are there! You won't go far just hoping someone will spot your new sign when driving along the road. Advertising in the local free papers, county papers, national papers is one way – but you really need to be seen looking professional. These days there are so many craft shows, weekly markets, horse shows, charity fairs, Christmas fairs, boot sales, exhibitions, county shows that offer good opportunities. Whatever you are selling, there will be many places where you can set up a stall, display your wares, and hand out your leaflets.

Any kind of herb product attracts interest, and, although exhausting sometimes, it can be great fun and profitable too. There is great satisfaction after a busy day at a fair, to sit down with a heavy cash tin at the kitchen table and count the takings! If you enjoy selling your herbs, and know they are good, people will enjoy buying them, and find their way to your nursery to see what else you have in stock.

Aiming at the right level

This may seem obvious, but is still worth mentioning. Small plants at lower prices are best at a county show – not many people want to stagger round with a large 'planted up' terra-cotta pot. Christmas gift fairs require pretty packaging and seasonal culinary herbs (Parsley, Rosemary etc). Extra-large plants, well-displayed on the nursery, sell well to gardeners who have moved house and want an instant, usable and attractive herb garden.

Open days, group visits

To avoid the constant repetition of 'we didn't know you were there', remember the value of putting your nursery on show for an 'Open Day', perhaps in aid of a special local charity. Enlist the help of the charity committee to help the day run smoothly and suggest either a small charge at the 'gate' or collecting boxes and teas. Put plenty of posters around and let the local press know about it in good time – then pray for good weather! Even if it pours with rain and only six people arrive, your nursery will stay immaculate for weeks! Encourage gardening clubs and women's groups to visit you for their summer outings. If they enjoy themselves, your reputation will be spread by word of mouth, and soon you will be booked a year or more ahead by similarly interested groups of people.

Observation, initiative, energy and enthusiasm will all help to overcome obstacles, but knowing when to look and listen will teach you more about customers and markets in the end.

How much shall I charge?

One of the most common questions asked by the newcomer to herb growing is 'How much should I charge for my products?' The question is meaningless unless you know how much it is costing to produce them. I know the easiest way is to 'look over the fence' and see what others are charging, but are you sure that your neighbour is right, and making sufficient profit to remain in business? At some time in the future you will probably produce something unique, and there will be no pricing guide to help you. If you build up a record of your outgoings from the start it is a simple matter to apply some of the known costs immediately, and only have the unknown ones to estimate.

It doesn't matter on what scale you are working, if you are going to effect sales you need to have confidence in your asking price, otherwise you may, on impulse, agree to sell at a lower price than at first intended only to find it hard to make ends meet.

Producing bunches of dried herb flowers in festive arrangements for a Christmas fair with all the profits going to a worthy cause or charity needs accurate costing of the materials, so that the donor is not out of pocket. The cost of the time taken in gathering the material and making the arrangement is not usually charged – that is the maker's gift to the charity. This represents a valuable donation, because if charged at an adequate rate per hour the retail selling price probably would not prove tempting enough to sell many items.

It is very essential to understand two simple terms, in order to price your herbs.

Fixed costs

These are costs which will be there whether you actually sell any products or not. Usually they will include *regular* labour (as well as your own, of course, and don't forget that you will have to pay someone else to do your work if you are absent), general maintenance, administration, insurance and rates etc.

Variable costs

These costs alter according to the sales, ie the more pot sales, the more pots to be purchased. Labour on a casual basis or employed only on a particular product becomes a variable cost.

Typical variable costs which can apply to production of pot plants

(a) Pots or containers, suitable for the type of sale and length of life of the plant before sale.

(b) Propagation trays, costs of heating.

(c) Compost materials (remember time and labour cost if home-mixed).

(d) Trays for transporting pots.

(e) Labels.

(f) Materials for standing beds.

(g) Carrier bags, boxes or packaging materials.

(h) Labour costs, calculated by the time multiplied by the

wages rate per hour that it takes to produce the plant at point of sale. These will include:

Compost mixing	Selling, if retail outlet
Preparing plants	Propagation
Moving plants to	Potting
standing ground	Watering
Feeding plants if	Moving plants to sales area
necessary	Trimming
Labelling	Delivery, if wholesale outlet

Having considered all the foregoing it is then always wise to add a little extra somewhere to cover all contingencies.

Materials are simple to identify for costing, but labour is the variable that can be the hidden high cost. If paying your staff on an hourly basis, examine just how efficient is the use of time on your nursery. This variable cost can be controlled, whereas fixed costs are difficult to reduce.

If you can calculate the cost per pot, or per hundred pots, then a sensible selling price may be set, which will show you a profit. Too many nurserymen forget to cost the time taken on apparently small tasks like trimming, labelling, moving plants (the latter can be expensive in time). Again, the use of too small a pot, which soon has to be potted on if not sold immediately, reduces your profit.

If labour represents 60 per cent of your gross profit you have a problem. If labour is less than 30 per cent of your gross profit, please tell me the secret of your methods, because you must be making a good profit! Remember gross profit minus fixed costs and variable costs equals net profit.

In setting a value on your product, think what is the 'perceived' value – what would you be prepared to pay for it? A value judgement is automatically set to work in one's mind when deciding whether to buy or not. Is your value judgement good? Do you agree with the current price of products which are similar to your own? It is a hard, but essential, lesson to learn that you cannot sell profitably if you are inefficient.

This brings us once again to where we started – your prospective customers. Stop and think about the people who will be most important to your enterprise.

9
Organizing a business

Do not let the title of this chapter put you off reading it even if you are one of the many who get mental indigestion at the idea of 'book keeping'. I assure you that it can be enjoyable, if you don't allow yourself to take fright at the thought of Bought ledgers, eighteen-column analysis books, computer print-outs and so on. Tell yourself that this is only 'terminology' and once you have a system going that is understandable to you and your accountant, you will have a temperature record of your business and can decide quickly whether it is ill or bouncing with health.

Anyone who has a liking for order, figures, pristine financial records, and a natural feeling for administration will read my list of essentials and notice all the things I don't do. I confess that I am a reluctant office worker, and do not keep records and books for their own sake.

For those of you about to start a business (and don't fool yourself, growing herbs professionally on any scale is a business), then initially all the paperwork will be done by you. If you set up simple, workable systems in the beginning, then you can delegate with confidence as soon as your business expands sufficiently. If you enjoy paperwork, then remain in the warm office and happily watch everyone else outside on a cold winter day. Don't forget though that you may also be in that office during the long, beautiful days of summer!

For information and help on setting up a business, contact CoSira, Small Firms Service (see p.151), who can advise on all aspects. For information on book-keeping, VAT, etc, contact your local Department of Employment who have devised several informative leaflets.

The following paragraphs illustrate my own system which has proved entirely satisfactory.

Daily Routine

Deal with all the incoming mail, remember to stamp everything with the date received.

Large waste paper baskets

This is for all the envelopes, circulars, repeat statements (not bank), unsolicited offers, trade offers (unless you really want them now or in the future). Also into the WPB should go all the old trade magazines, unless you have someone to whom you can give them. Don't have a staggering pile waiting to be read 'when you have time', unless you really have got spare time! Cut out anything really relevant to keep on a ring file and discard the rest.

New files

These are essential so that you can immediately open a file for a new customer or subject. This avoids bits of paper and letters clipped together and lost in all the other bits of paper! You will then fall into the habit of 'paper shuffling'. This looks busy if anyone comes in, but is a total waste of time and a source of great irritation when an item is needed quickly.

Box files

For me, necessary office equipment; mine are used for:

(1) *Accountant.* This is for paid bills with date of payment and cheque number written on the invoice, VAT forms, books of cheque stubs and bank pay-in books, strange demands from the Inland Revenue, and anything else financial that I think he needs to see, or that I do not understand.

(2) *Unpaid bills.* At least they all stay in one place. In theory all advice and delivery notes go in here too, but these start life on a larger clip for everyone to add to each day. Also on

this clip are petrol and petty cash slips (stationery, stamps, sundries etc) so that they should (in theory) stay in date order.

(3) *Letters requiring a reply.* Again, I should be able to find them all when the free moment and inspiration arrive. It is a good idea to quickly draft a rough answer to each letter on first reading, by writing on it in note form the information to be contained in your reply. It refreshes the memory when you actually come to do it and saves a lot of time. My box tends to get clogged with all the difficult letters that require more thought and research.

(4) *Bank Box.* Not labelled as this, but in our office it has mysterious initials denoting those who use it. Into this box go current and new cheque books, current pay-in books, cheques to be entered into the bank ledger before banking, and daily petty cash slips to be collated into weeks. Do not tuck cheques behind clocks, under books or leave in envelopes. They are much safer paid into the bank and cleared!

Card files

It is good sense to keep card files of customers. This makes for easy and quick reference and enables family and staff to answer queries intelligently.

Sales and Bought Ledgers

I keep two ledgers, which could be labelled simply 'In' and 'Out'. These two are essential and for this purpose I use good long-lasting attractive multi-ring binders, containing sheets with the number of columns I need and which are obtainable in standard replacement packs.

Keeping records in an old exercise book is not good psychology, I find. If I have paid good, hard-earned money for Sales and Bought ledgers they are entered neatly and kept up to date. Only by analysing what you buy can you actually obtain a basis for costing your final product.

The Sales ledger is entered from consecutively numbered

invoice books – easily obtainable from stationers. Each customer has a separate page, however few the entries may be. At first sight this may sound unnecessary work, but read on! This system means that you will not require yet another book for sending statements (I hope that you are not naïve enough to believe that everyone pays on time). The relevant pages of the ledger are detached and photocopied as the money becomes overdue and these copies are sent out as reminders. (I have now purchased a photocopier but initially used the services of our local estate agent's machine.) Somehow it does jog people's memories and conscience when the whole page is laid before them, rather than a flat statement which then has to be checked.

Customers' unpaid bills

Regarding these, it is your money, so chase it if necessary! Cash in the hand is great, but with any small business a lot will depend on its potential customers, who will have their own established pattern of making payments. Computers are the scourge of small businesses, and payments from large customers are often delayed, nearly always hiding somewhere in the computerized accounts department. If really pushed, such firms will nearly always agree to bring payments forward on a shorter time basis – or, as I told one company secretary when I was about to refuse further supplies, someone could always pick up a pen and manually issue a cheque! Make sure that you are sending invoices to the correct address for payment. Many multiple firms have their accounts department at a quite separate address from their production units.

With new customers, do ascertain and agree the method of payment and any time delay involved – it might affect your quotation. The longer the delay in obtaining what is in fact your money, the greater resentment you will feel – and that does not make for good customer relationships.

Paying your own bills

If you can, do pay your bills on time, especially if a discount is available. This will definitely build you up a sound 'track record' and will help if you have to provide credit references when first ordering from a large firm and opening a credit account. Integrity may be an old-fashioned word, but it still counts for something in the business world, however cynical some people may be!

Time

The mail is dealt with, bills paid, files put away, cheques entered – you are free to start your day, but what usually happens? The telephone rings constantly, representatives and customers call, deliveries are made, customers' questions are answered and time melts away . . .

Telephone

I know that it can be irritating to be constantly interrupted – but please don't let it show when you answer! Even if you force a smile it does show in your voice, you never know who may be calling! Keep a flip pad by the telephone for business only (not scraps of paper used by all the family). Then you will be able to refer back and refresh your memory when trying to sort out a revised order. Keep a current duplicate order book, so that if your top copy gets wet with spilled coffee, or is blown out of your hand there is still a record available.

Representatives

Make friends with your regular good 'reps'; their work is interesting and essential to you. Then on the days when you are too busy to do more than thrust an order at them or say 'no' they will understand. I know that a lot of people will not see 'reps', but I have learned so much from their long association with growers, spiced with a bit of enjoyable trade gossip, that I would like to express my gratitude to them. If you always remember that there are real people like yourself at each end of every transaction, no matter how complicated the chain, you won't go far wrong.

Finance

Bank managers

Don't take fright at the thought of dealing with these people, who are so important to your business. If you have a sound, well-thought-out and researched plan to show your bank manager, when turning your hobby into a business, then make an appointment and enjoy it! Only the rash, foolhardy type of person tries to fool a good manager with grandiose schemes and no market, or with wildly optimistic plans about unrealistic outputs from small areas. It concentrates the mind wonderfully if you have need to finance a business and must produce evidence to support your case! If you are thoroughly convinced you are offering a good plan, go in with confidence and flags flying! Do not close your ears to all the points he has to make: if necessary go away and think carefully before returning with the answers. Do not feel compelled to stay with the bank you have dealt with for years; managers vary in their attitude to certain types of business. Horticulture is not lucrative and tends to need solid overdrafts. Banks offer advisory services, take advantage of them – they are usually free.

Accountants

These people can be rather intimidating to small business folk, so it is preferable to deal with a good independent one who will take an interest in what you are doing and in how the business progresses. Dumping a large box of papers on a busy firm of accountants once a year, and then waiting for six months for results which by that time seem irrelevant is not wise. It is surprising how many people do just that, and consequently lose touch with the realities of the financial side of their business.

Example of a simple plan for a bank manager:
(figures given are very simple for clarity).
Proposal A small garden centre concentrating on herbs and cottage garden plants. Open from 10am – 5pm, March to September. Closed in winter to build up stock.

Assets Half hectare of land, old greenhouse in fair condition. Good access from a busy road. Past history of use as bedding-plant nursery. Some useful equipment, although rather run down. Existing buildings, and a sign by the road. Owners retiring.

Research Local garden centres have limited herb sections, no one specializing in herbs in area. No planning problems, no objection locally, mainly interest and support.

Resources An increasing interest in growing herbs. Horticultural training (anything that will back up your reasons for going in for herbs and horticulture). Enough knowledge to advise customers. Sufficient time to undertake running a business. Husband will keep his job until the profit is sufficient (and he is very good at renovations and building).

Estimated costs at their highest limit

Repairs	£1000
Small polythene tunnel house	800
Stock plants and seeds	500
Compost and pots etc	1000
Tools, barrows, benching etc	400
Telephone, sundry items, interest	800
	£4500

Capital available	£3000
Loan required	£1500

Estimated sales at lowest projected figure for first season

6000 plants @ 50p	£3000
2000 plants @ £1.00	2000
2000 plants @ £2.00	4000
Sundry other sales	500
	£9500

Cost of extra labour at peak times	£2000
Gross profit	£7500

On this basis, it might be advisable to ask for a working overdraft, as you would probably be able to pay the money back over one season, with enough left over to take some pocket money and restock. If you are dependent on the income, then perhaps a loan over several years is necessary. It all depends on the advice given and your own financial situation.

Even if it does not quite work out the way that you intended, at least you will start with a financial plan that can be examined and altered for the following season.

Hopefully in the first season there would not be a loss and a decision could be made on how to continue. The next year should show greatly increased sales as you gain experience and become known.

Self-training

This is not an easy subject to assess in a few words, but there are many cassette tapes and courses available if one wishes to analyse oneself to improve 'self management'. Even if you are intending to do all the work by yourself, it does help to introduce some method into your life unless you are already a born organizer!

When you first require extra workers, unless you are one of the rare natural employers you may find yourself doing all the dull and trivial jobs while Janet or Jim sit happily at the propagating bench! It is only too easy to fall into the 'it's easier to do it myself than explain' trap. It may take a bit of time initially to think out a method which will achieve the maximum output possible in a working day, in the least tiring and most satisfactory way, but it will pay off in the end.

I feel that I have learned most about self-training through the Agricultural Training Board courses on Man Management. I recommend in particular a 'Decision Making' type of course. The one I attended for two days cleared a whole thicket of ancient, dusty cobwebs from my brain. The idea behind management courses should now be familiar to us all. Large firms in particular as well as many smaller ones have come to realize the value of time and money spent on training.

Efficient use of time

A few years ago I enlisted the professional business services of a friend to assess the potential of the herb farm and to suggest improvements. The final analysis was that I was wasting my time! After the initial shock and resistance, I realized how right he was – and our friendship has survived and prospered. To quote from one of his articles: 'Time, everyone has it in equal measure, but the art of success is to put it to its best advantage.'

The herb farm was improving each year and the number of customers increasing, but my time was overfilled and hectic. Why? To quote him again: 'Time robbers.' These include paper shuffling, lack of delegation, putting off decisions, talking too much, an inability to say 'no', guilty feelings, people who want free advice. Even working in too 'cosy' a setting can slow down essential paper work. Work expands to fill the time available, so setting a time limit is necessary.

We all have our personal list of 'time wasters' and there are always a few that we do not want to part with. The important point is to recognize them for what they are, and if you enjoy talking to a friend on the telephone for half an hour in the middle of a working day, then count that as leisure, and don't feel frustrated because at the end of the day your work is not completed.

Being self-employed requires more stringent self-discipline than when working for someone else – but if you keep your sense of humour it's great fun.

Youth Employment

Government schemes come and go, but the basic dilemma remains – how can young school-leavers obtain training and experience in all types of work, in order to make a more balanced, adult decision about their future? There have been some well-thought-out schemes in the past which worked efficiently and were simple to administer. At present most of us in horticulture have had or will have dealings with the Youth Training Scheme (YTS), which bases most of the formal training on the two days a week spent away from the working place at an agricultural or horticultural college.

My own attitude towards these various schemes is that I try to fit in with the current philosophy, but I make sure that all the rules and regulations help, not hinder, a young worker. It always takes a little time for under-used muscles to respond, and for the attitude of the young person to alter as he or she discovers that it is quite possible to work with people of all ages. They come to realize that we are not in the role of teachers or parents, but part of a working team, with each person contributing to the whole output of the nursery, on which they might depend for the security of their job should they decide to remain with us.

I cannot say that all the youngsters who have come to us have been successful in horticulture, or would wish to take it up as a career. Their time with us is not always trouble-free, mostly personal problems concerning their relationships with adults! They *can* become very useful extra workers on the nursery, and we try to give them confidence and new skills in return. The Government subsidy helps to compensate for the time taken on training and dealing with problems, and many trainees progress into formal or informal apprentices, becoming valuable workers.

Advice on the most recent subsidies or grants, training schemes and other benefits available, can be obtained from the Ministry of Agriculture, Fisheries and Food. Of course, your accountant will be able to discuss all the options with you, and help you decide the most beneficial course of action.

10

Coping with problems

Don't panic – fortunately herbs are fairly trouble-free plants, if they are growing well and in a situation that is natural to them. Problems tend to arise when we grow plants in an artificial environment – glass and polythene houses, low tunnels, or large areas of one type of plant. The need to extend the natural season early and late in the year by growing under cover, in order to supply the demand from customers, can exacerbate the problems.

Daily observation is the key to dealing with pest and disease problems, so that you detect the symptoms in the early stages. In time one develops a 'grower's eye', and any change in leaf colour, or an alteration in growth alerts one to inspect more closely.

Not every sneeze leads to influenza, so don't panic and think of major disasters every time things look different. Check for simple, obvious causes first – is it weather damage: excessive rain over a long period, which causes waterlogging at the roots? Is it the effect of frost – die-back of new shoots, purpling of the margins of some leaves, death of others? If there are dead shoots, could it be mechanical damage (machinery or large feet)? Check for pests and try to identify them.

How you solve all these problems is dependent on your particular outlook and method of growing, using organic or chemical methods. Obviously, if the problem is waterlogged soil then the question of adequate drainage will have to be investigated. If it is frost and general weather damage, then are the crops in the best place to avoid the worst of the weather? Should you be considering low tunnels, windbreaks, or changing your future planting schemes? Each nursery is a law unto itself, and only experience will show you how to use your land and assets to the best advantage.

Please don't imagine that everything goes smoothly and perfectly on my nursery. I still see problems as a Hydra, a multi-headed monster. As soon as one problem is solved, another one pops up – but I remain philosophical about these things. Experience is a great teacher, and we are constantly researching and trying out new ideas.

The winter of 1986 was a most difficult one, with extended cold and wet spells. Everything was about three weeks behind, fuel bills were still arriving, there was mud everywhere and the land was too wet to work. However, a few days of sunshine and growing weather and optimism increases. One can get down to some hard work and try to catch up on existing and new planting plans. Who would want to be shut indoors when you can almost hear things growing in the garden.

There is much advice to be found in the plethora of good gardening and herb books, on how to deal with pests and diseases. The Ministry of Agriculture, Fisheries and Food publishes an excellent series of leaflets on particular problems; most are free, and the address to write to is given on page 151. It is a good idea to build up a file of material on the subject of problem solving, and then to make good use of it.

There are so many chemical remedies for pest and disease attacks, that I do not feel able to give specific names of materials. So few are cleared for use on herbs, their being a minority interest for the large firms, who run trials and obtain clearance for using certain chemicals on edible crops.

Pest and Diseases

When these problems appear, don't panic – apply common

sense. If your plants do not look healthy, examine them for tell-tale signs; it may be quite simple to find a solution, perhaps it is merely a case of lack of feed or too much fertilizer used at one time.

If there is a poor general appearance and stunted growth and pale leaves, then check for root damage. This may be caused by the roots being waterlogged due to over-watering and bad drainage, or being too dry because of a lack of water and compacted soil or compost. Root damage can also be the result of bad planting, sciriad fly, slugs, snails, carrot fly or mealy bug. Become familiar with pests (if only on a theoretical basis), so that you can recognize them when they appear.

Publications for amateurs can be very useful. The Royal Horticultural Society and many popular gardening magazines have all produced excellent booklets and wall charts in recent years. Pin the chart up in your potting shed, examine the damage with a good magnifying glass and compare it with the photographs. If a pest – say pollen beetle – is recognized, look over your boundary hedges. If your neighbouring farmer has flowering oil seed rape, pollen beetle may well be migrating to all yellow and orange flowers in your nursery.

If the leaves are ragged, have small holes or pale 'trails', then it is clearly pest damage. Look for the obvious culprits first, such as slugs, snails, caterpillars, birds or rabbits, before you leap to the use of chemicals.

Leaves that have tiny pale spots may be infested with red spider mite, thrips or leaf hoppers, in which case biological control is one answer. An insect predator can also be used if whitefly is found on stock plants. This is difficult to control once it takes hold in a greenhouse. The firms supplying the predators also give advice on how to use them. Addresses of suppliers can be found on page 156.

Powdery mildew – dry, grey powdery spots – tends to appear in dry conditions while botrytis – a mould which rots the leaves – tends to appear in wet, damp conditions.

If analysing the problem and applying the correct deterrent were simple, then pest and disease control would not be the multi-million-pound industry it is today. But please don't think you are going to meet all these problems at the same time. I have mentioned a few of the most common ones; the solutions depend on the type of growing you practise, and on your good relationships with advisory services, exchange of information with other growers, and your own common sense.

On a small scale, there are many sprays available from any good garden centre which will cope with most of the aforementioned problems. If in doubt, stick to the non-systemic types. On a larger scale, horticultural sundriesmen have a great deal of experience and can offer good advice on the types of chemicals available.

For organic growers the Soil Association has a list of permitted sprays and fertilizers, the Henry Doubleday Institute provides information and publications, and there are books on companion planting now available (see page 153 for further information and addresses.)

Winter income

If you are totally dependent on the income from your enterprise, the subject of winter income looms large. Of course, if you are a perfect financial manager, who can stick to forward cash flows (and make them match), you will aim to produce your winter income during the most financially rewarding months of the year and then manage over the 'dead' ones. This latter time can then be utilized for holidays, seeing more of the family, and catching up with the hundred and one jobs that have been put to one side in the busy times. The other main objective at this time would be to complete all planning etc for the following season: placing seed and plant orders, effecting machinery repairs, training – anything which can be done in good time to allow your mind to be free to cope with the busy season ahead. Much depends on which type of herb enterprise you are engaged in, and on what scale.

Fresh herbs

Fresh herbs may be kept as a seasonal venture, with your customers understanding this and obtaining their winter supplies elsewhere. Imported herbs offer better prices during our difficult growing season and I have not yet found it cost-effective to grow more than emergency crops for winter, when one has to compete with these cheaper supplies from more favourable climes. My own solution has been to link with a source in a Mediterranean country, advising and instigating some of the crops to be grown, so that we both may benefit from mutual co-operation without spoiling each other's markets. As time goes by I hope that this venture will become well enough established so that there can be some kind of marketing/supply information service which will ensure that herbs are available at prices which will benefit everyone – grower, supplier, consumer alike. Too many 'middle men' minimizes the profit for those actually doing most of the work!

Dried herbs

Obviously those in large-scale growing will already have budgeted for their winter incomes. Smaller-scale growers, who depend on direct sales to the public with dried herbs and gift items, should explore the delightful world of gift fairs (or fayres!), Christmas bazaars, craft exhibitions, and mail order. If you have produced something unusual or topical, a cleverly worded advertisement or a mention in an editorial can produce a quite surprising response. Be prepared for anything, but don't be downhearted if it doesn't work first time. Try to analyse what went wrong. Was it timing, wording, readership, or the Cup Final? Even a crisis in the headlines can affect impulse buying. One cannot always get it right – but it can keep things moving during the winter.

Talks, courses, lectures

This is another traditional way of using the long dark evenings profitably. But do please make sure that you have something to say! If you are a nervous speaker, then it is worth while and very interesting to go to a course on public speaking.

It will help with so many minor problems – one being how to breathe correctly so that your voice will come out confidently and firmly, even if your knees are shaking. Try when offering yourself (or accepting an offer) as speaker to a group, to give your talk an interesting and intriguing title, not just 'HERBS by Mrs . . . ' Take one aspect of whatever your main interest is, and on which you have most knowledge, and present the whole talk as interestingly as possible, with plenty of samples to keep your hands busy – and hopefully to sell later! There is always something to learn from each new audience, and sometimes you will find their knowledge is more extensive than your own. If you do well, your fame will spread and your name will become firmly established on every group secretary's list for future reference when they are compiling their programmes of talks for the winter.

II

Amateur or professional?

There are brilliant amateurs, and amateurish professionals, so how does one define all the grey areas in between – and where shall we place ourselves? Herbs are such a topic of public fascination, that the progression from the delight of growing for oneself, into growing to sell to others is becoming widespread. At some point a time is reached when it is necessary to take stock of one's personal abilities and assets. Usually this occurs when a major change is envisaged – a move to the country for more space, redundancy, return from working abroad, the need for a second income as children grow, early retirement. The change in lifestyle is justified by the desire to grow herbs in some way, and make a profit. Real honesty is needed now, before another muddled herbiary is born!

How much do you really know about herbs?
The time to remedy any lack of knowledge is now, while there is still time to visit herb gardens and plant specialists, to read widely and sift facts, study exhibitions etc. Try working in horticulture if possible, or go on short horticultural courses; practise plant recognition and new ways of using herbs. A good, sound, basic knowledge will help tremendously. Don't worry, no-one knows 'all' about herbs; it would be foolish to

believe that there comes a point when there is nothing more to be discovered. You need to know more than the average customer, otherwise how can you gain their respect and enhance your reputation when the questions start pouring in. In garden centres, people enjoy wandering around and being left to select and pay at the check-out. Herb customers love to talk about herbs and ask questions. Chefs and caterers expect you to understand their requirements for a continual supply of accurate herbs. Everyone expects value for money!

Enjoy growing herbs to sell. Try to start with one main objective and gradually introduce new enterprises when the first plan has stabilized.

Are your family really 'with you' – or do they regard it as yet another mad hobby?

Not all your children or relatives will be sympathetic to your chosen lifestyle, because it is certainly nothing like a 9am to 5pm regular job, with weekends free and holidays paid! If you are overwhelmed by joyful helpers with green fingers and non-mercenary natures, then you can skip the next few lines. On the other hand, some teenage children can become actively hostile, unless an obviously large profit is being made (and shared)! Being self-employed and growing herbs can be a time- and energy-consuming business, which may cause the other members of the family to feel left out and neglected. There may be a marked reluctance to offer assistance – paid or unpaid, and this is not unusual.

A happy knowledgeable 'amateur' making a part-time income out of herbs, which are grown and sold in a professional way, may be a wise compromise for many people.

Competition

A striking change takes place when you alter status and decide to become a professional – those who have previously been involved in any business will readily understand this point. You have stepped round to the other side of the counter, and people become customers, competitors and critics!

The act of paying money appears to give licence to some individuals to discuss plants, gifts, herb products – even yourself – as though you were not personally present. I am always amused at the number of rational, pleasant people who feel it quite normal to take up my working time, and expect me to give advice on how to set up in opposition, even expecting names of customers!

Herb growing is a competitive business, and you must remember that you will be in competition with already established growers, as well as many others who are planning to grow herbs commercially in the near future.

One way to overcome this potentially lonely and hostile situation is to join a trade organization. The British Herb Trade Association was formed for this purpose in 1976 (see p.151). There are plenty of opportunities and room for newcomers, and one is able to co-operate with others of a like mind in discussions of common problems, on coping with gluts and shortages, in learning from research and experience. Meetings are held regionally and nationally throughout the year, with member nurseries playing host. Marketing conferences, regular newsletters, a reference map for the public, joint publicity, seminars on many topics – these are just a few of the many items which can be achieved by joint co-operation, and are so difficult for individuals to cope with.

The most important point of all is to be completely honest with yourself. Answer the following brief questionnaire for fun; it is designed to make you think and help you make some fundamental decisions before you embark.

1. How much do you really know about herbs and commercial
   growing?
   - (a) a lot ☐
   - (b) quite a lot ☐
   - (c) not much ☐

2. Why do you want to grow them professionally?
   - (a) profit ☐
   - (b) modest return ☐
   - (c) not bothered about cash ☐

3. Have you a ready market for herbs?
   - (a) big market ready and waiting ☐
   - (b) already sold a few, people interested ☐
   - (c) want to jump on the band wagon ☐

4. Do you know which area of herb growing you prefer?
   - (a) yes ☐
   - (b) thought I'd copy the nursery next door ☐
   - (c) no ☐

5. Have you money to invest that you can afford to lose or to
   have little immediate return?
   - (a) yes ☐
   - (b) prepared to lose a little while gaining
     experience ☐
   - (c) can't lose, with the present 'boom'
     in the market ☐

6. Do you have original ideas?
   - (a) yes ☐
   - (b) can use and improve on other people's ☐
   - (c) no need; herbs sell themselves; people
     will flock to my door ☐

7. Can you do the paperwork and cost enterprises?

    (a) yes ☐

    (b) will learn ☐

    (c) why do I need to? ☐

8. Are you on friendly terms with your bank manager?

    (a) yes ☐

    (b) no ☐

    (c) don't need him ☐

9. Is your family 'with you' on the idea of herb growing?

    (a) yes ☐

    (b) they tolerate it ☐

    (c) no ☐

It doesn't need a professional analyst to tell you that if all your answers are from the 'c' section it would be wise to think again, but would a 'c' person listen?

If all 'b's, then the problems could be solved. Obviously you are a realistic person with initiative.

If all 'a's, and everything sounds perfect, are you perhaps in danger of being overconfident?!

Your final question to yourself should be: if I am successful can I stand the strain, and if I am unsuccessful can I stand the financial loss?

To conclude, if I have managed to provoke thought and discussion with this book, then I feel I shall have achieved my objectives. Whatever you decide to do, I hope you will always enjoy and convey to others the pleasure of growing herbs.

Appendix

HERB GARDENS TO VISIT IN THE BRITISH ISLES

England

Avon	American Museum, Bath The Dower House, Badminton Orchard House, Claverton, Bath
Berkshire	Hollington Nurseries, Woolton Hill, Newbury The Old Vicarage, Bucklebury
Cambridgeshire	The Botanic Gardens, Cambridge Emmanuel College, Cambridge
Cheshire	Arley Estate Office, Northwich Little Moreton Hall, Nr Congleton
Cornwall	County Demonstration Garden, Probus Polsue Cottage Herbs, Truro
Cumbria	Acorn Bank Garden, Temple Sowerby, Penrith
Derbyshire	Elvaston Castle, County Park, Borrowash Road, Elvaston Hardwick Hall, Nr Chesterfield
Devon	Castle Drogo, Drewsteignton Dartington Hall, Totnes The Old Barn, Fremington, Barnstaple

Dorset	Dean's Court, Wimborne
	Highbury, Nr Wimborne
	The Manor Gardens, Cranborne
	The Red House Museum, Quay Road, Christchurch
East Sussex	Bateman's, Burwash
	Michelham Priory Physic Garden, Upper Dicker, Nr Hailsham
Gloucestershire	Barnsley House, Nr Cirencester
	Hidcote Manor, Nr Chipping Campden
	Selsley Herb and Goat Farm, Selsley, Nr Stroud
	Westbury Court, Westbury-on-Severn
Hampshire	Beaulieu Abbey Cloisters
	Butser Ancient Farm Research Project, Rookham Lodge, East Meon
	Curtis Museum & Allen Gallery, Swanmore
	Longstock Park Gardens, Stockbridge
	Mechellmersh Court, Romsey
	Tudor Museum, Southampton
	West Green House, Hartley Wintney
Hereford & Worcester	Abbey Dore Court, Hereford
	Stoke Lacey Herb Garden, Bromyard
Hertfordshire	Capel Manor Institute of Horticulture, Waltham Cross
	Hatfield House, Hatfield
	Knebworth House, Knebworth
	The Manor House, Chenies, Rickmansworth
Kent	Eyhorne Manor, Hollingbourne
	The Herb Garden, Spots Farm, Small-hythe, Tenterden

Hever Castle, Nr Edenbridge
Iden Croft Herbs, Frittenden Road, Staplehurst
Knole, Sevenoaks
Scotney Castle Gardens, Lamberhurst, Tunbridge Wells
Sissinghurst Castle Gardens, Sissinghurst, Cranbrook
Stoneacre, Offham, Nr Maidstone
Withersdane Hall, Nr Ashford

Leicestershire	Cosby House, Cosby Newarke House Museum, Leicester Stone Cottage, Hambleton University of Leicester Botanic Gardens
Lincolnshire	Gunby Hall, Burgh-le-Marsh Lincoln Cathedral Gardens
London	Chelsea Physic Garden Fulham Palace Gardens Greenwich Park Westminster Abbey College Gardens
Merseyside	University of Liverpool Botanic Gardens, Neston, South Wirral
Norfolk	Felbrigg Hall, Roughton Norfolk Lavender Ltd, Heacham, King's Lynn Oxburgh Hall, Swaffham
Nottinghamshire	Holme Pierrepont Hall, Nottingham South Collingham House, Collingham
Oxfordshire	Marndhill, Ardington, Troy Ewelme W.I. Education Centre, Denham College, Marcham, Nr Abingdon
Shropshire	Mawley Hall, Cleobury Mortimer

	Oak Cottage Herb Farm, Nesscliff
Somerset	East Lambrook Manor, South Petherton
	Gaulden Manor, Tolland
	R.T. Herbs, Kilmersdon
Staffordshire	The Bradshaws, Wrottesley
Suffolk	Gainsborough's House, Sudbury
	Netherfield Herbs, Nether Street, Rougham
Surrey	The Herb Garden, Kew Gardens
	The Royal Horticultural Society's Garden, Wisley
West Midlands	Moseley Old Hall, Wolverhampton
	Queen's Park, Harborne, Birmingham (Fragrance Garden for the Blind)
	Urban Herbs, 91 Clifton Road, Balsall Heath, Birmingham
West Sussex	Clock House, Denmans, Fontwell, Nr Arundel
	Cooke's House, West Burton
Wiltshire	Hillbarn House, Great Bedwyn
	Lackham College of Agriculture
Yorkshire	Abbey House Museum, Leeds
	York Gate, Adel, Leeds

Channel Islands

Samares Herbs a Plenty,
St Clement, Jersey

Ireland

Spring Hill, County Londonderry
Donaghmore House, Ballygarrett,
Gorey, County Wexford

Scotland

The Edinburgh Botanic Gardens'
Edinburgh
Findhorn Foundation, Forres
Glasgow Botanic Gardens, Glasgow
Netherbyres, Nr Eyemouth,
Berwickshire
Old Semeil Herb Garden, Strathdon
Threave Garden, Castle Douglas,
Dumfries & Galloway

Wales

Bible Garden, Bangor
St Fagan's Garden, Cardiff

Note

The foregoing is a selection of the many herb gardens in Britain
which are open to the public. A list of the herb farms and
nurseries, many of which have demonstration gardens, is
available from The Herb Society.

Agricultural Development and Advisory Service (ADAS), Great Westminster House, Horseferry Road, London SW1P 2AE

Agricultural Training Board, ATB Training Centre, NAC, Kenilworth, Warwickshire CV8 2LG

British Herb Trade Association, Administrator, BHTA, c/o The National Farmers' Union, Agriculture House, 25-31 Knightsbridge, London SW1X 7NJ. Map available showing location of herb farms, plant nurseries, gardens etc. in Britain (50p by post).

British Standards Institution, 2 Park Street, London W1A 2BS

CoSira (Council for Small Industries in Rural Areas), 141 Castle Street, Salisbury, Wilts SP1 3TP. Look in telephone directory for nearest local branch.

The Cookery and Food Association of Great Britain, Miss M. Shepherd, 1 Victoria Parade, by 331 Sandycombe Road, Richmond, Surrey TW9 3NB

Electricity Council's Farm-electric Centre, National Agricultural Centre, Stoneleigh, Kenilworth, Warwickshire CV8 2LS. Write for list of free publications for farmers and growers.

Henry Doubleday Research Institute, Ryton-on-Dunsmore, Coventry, CV8 3LG

The Herbal Treatment Centre, 65 Frant Road, Tunbridge Wells, Kent TN2 5EY

The Cookery and Food Association of Great Britain, Miss M. Shepherd, 1 Victoria Parade, by 331 Sandycombe Road, Richmond, Surrey TW9 3NB

Ministry of Agriculture, Fisheries and Food, Great Westminster House, Horseferry Road, London SW1A 2HH. Publications Dept: Lion House, Willowburn Estate, Alnwick, Northumberland NE66 2PF

National Council for the Conservation of Plants and Gardens, c/o RHS Gardens, Wisley, Woking, Surrey GU23 6QB

National Farmers' Union, Agriculture House, 25-31 Knightsbridge, London SW1X 7NJ

The National Institute of Medical Herbalists, Hon. General Secretary, 41 Hatherley Road, Winchester, Hants SO22 6RR. Enclose a large sae for register of practitioners.

Small Firms Division, Department of Trade and Industry, Ashdown House, 123 Victoria Street, London SW1E 6RB or dial Freephone 2444 to contact your nearest centre

The Soil Association, Walnut Tree Manor, Haughley, Stowmarket, Suffolk IP14 3RS

Herb courses

Dates and venues alter from one year to the next. There are many advertized for amateurs, but few for the professionals!

Individual herb farms often offer special day courses to the public. If you finally intend to become a professional herb grower, much can be learned about the popular aspects of herbs from observation of your future customers. A list of herb farms and specialists offering courses may be obtained from The British Herb Trade Association, or from The Herb Society.

Colleges of Horticulture and Agriculture run courses for professional and amateur growers. It is worthwhile contacting your local college (to be found in the telephone directory) to see if anything is available to suit your requirements.

One-year postal courses and three- to four-year full-time courses in herbal medicine are available at the School of Herbal Medicine. Contact the Registrar at Bucksteep Manor, Bodle Street Green, Hailsham BN27 4RJ, tel (0323) 833812/4 for details.

Further reading

Bentham, G. and Hooker, D.D., *Handbook of the British Flora*, L. Reeve & Co., 1945

Bremness, Lesley, *The Herb Garden*, Sage Books, 1984

Brookes, John, *The Garden Book*, Dorling Kindersley, 1984

Chinnery, Michael, *The Living Garden*, Dorling Kindersley, 1986

David, Elizabeth, *Spices, Salts and Aromatics in the English Kitchen*, Penguin, 1970

Duff, Gail, *A Book of Pot-Pourri*, Orbis, 1985

Franck, Gertrud(e), *Companion Planting: Successful Gardening the Organic Way*, Thorsons, 1983

Garland, Sarah, *The Herb Garden*, Windward, 1984

Garland, Sarah, *The Herb and Spice Book*, Weidenfeld & Nicolson, 1979

Gerard, John, *The Herbal or General History of Plants*, 1633

Grieve, Maude and Leyel, Hilda, *A Modern Herbal*, Penguin, 1980

Groves, Eric, *Growing Herbs*, The Herb Society, 1977

Grower Books, 50 Doughty Street, London WC1N 2LP. Send for full book list specifically for growers.

HMSO, *Culinary and Medicinal Herbs*, 4th Edition, Reference Book 325, 1980

International Bee Research Organisation, Hill House, Gerrards Cross, Bucks SL9 0NR. *Garden Plants Valuable to Bees*, 1981

Martin, W. Keble, *The Concise British Flora*, Michael Joseph, 1965

Painter, Gilian, *A Herb Cook Book*, Hodder & Stoughton, 1983

Patterson, Alan, *Herbs in the Garden*, J.M. Dent, 1985

Peplow, Elizabeth, *Herbs and Herb Gardens*, Webb & Bower, 1984

Royal Horticultural Society, *Culinary Herbs*, Cassells, 1985

Sanecki, Kay N, *The Complete Book of Herbs*, The Apple Press, 1985

Stobart, Tom, *Herbs, Spices and Flavourings*, Penguin, 1977
Stuart, Malcolm (Ed.), *The Encyclopaedia of Herbs and Herbalism*, Orbis, 1979
Temple, Jack, *A Guide to Gardening Without Chemicals*, Thorsons, 1986
Tolley, Emelie and Mead, Chris, *Herbs, Gardens, Decorations and Recipes*, Sidgwick & Jackson, 1985
Toogood, Alan, *Propagation*, J.M. Dent, 1980
Verey, Rosemary, *The Scented Garden*, Mermaid Books, 1981

Other useful publications

Caterer and Hotel Keeper, Quadrant House, The Quadrant, Sutton, Surrey, SM2 5AS, or from large newsagents. Publishes 'Chef' Supplement.

The Grower, published by Grower Publications Ltd, 50 Doughty Street, London WC1N 2LP. Order from newsagents.

The Herbal Review, The Herb Society, 77 Great Peter Street, London SW1P 2EZ. Available quarterly for members.

Horticulture Week (formerly *Gardener's Chronicle & Horticultural Trade Journal*), Haymarket Publishing Ltd, 38/42 Hampton Road, Teddington, Middlesex TW11 0JE. Mail order.

Nurseryman and Garden Centre (Journal of the Horticultural Trades Association), Benn Publications Ltd, Sovereign Way, Tonbridge, Kent, TN9 1RW. Mail order. Useful for ideas for garden centre or large retail nursery.

'British Standards for container-grown herbs for culinary purposes' is published as Part II of BS3936 *Nursery Stock*, price £7.50, and is available from British Standards Sales Dept., Linford Wood, Milton Keynes, MK14 6AL and main Chambers of Commerce. Send cheque and *written* order.

Useful addresses

Herb plant suppliers (wholesale)

Addresses are also available from the British Herb Trade Association (*see* Useful organizations)

Anglia Alpines, Needington Road, Bluntisham, Huntingdon, Cambs PE17 3RJ

Binstead Herbs (through Fargro Ltd), The Old Rectory, Binstead, Sussex BN1 0LL

Hollington Nurseries Ltd, Woolton Hill, Newbury, Berks RG15 9XT

Peter Turner, Lighthorne Associates Ltd, Lighthorne Rough, Moreton Morrell, Warwickshire CV35 9DB

Rose Cottage Herbs, Acomb Common, Hatfield, Doncaster, S. Yorks DN7 6ET

Seed suppliers

Nutting & Speed Ltd, Long Stanton, Cambridge CB4 5BU

Suffolk Herbs, Sawyers Farm, Little Cornard, Sudbury, Suffolk CO10 0NY

C N Seeds, Denmark House, Pymoor, Ely, Cambs CB6 2EG

Dried herbs

Pierce A. Arnold & Son, Miami Works, Sandy Lane, North Wallington, Surrey SM6 8JX

Baldwins Ltd, 173 Walworth Road, London SE17

Brome & Schimmer Ltd, Greatbridge Road Estate, Romsey, Hants SO5 0HR

Norfolk Lavender Ltd, Caley Mill, Heacham, King's Lynn, Norfolk (lavender and gift products)

Micropropagation

Munton & Fison, plc, Cedars Factory, Stowmarket, Suffolk
IP14 2AG

Irrigation

Prime Waterman Ltd, Mere Farm Lane, Great Barton, Bury
St Edmunds, Suffolk IP31 2PH

Fragrances and essential oils etc

Aromatica International Ltd, Sealand Road, Chester CH1 4LP
Aromatica Oil Company, 12 Littlegate Street, Oxford OX1
1QT
John Bell & Croydon, 52–54 Wigmore Street, London W1H
9AU
Lothian Herbs, 45 Strathalmond Road, Edinburgh EH4 8HP

Horticultural sundries suppliers

Ffyffes Monro Horticultural Sundries Ltd, address in local
phone directory for nearest branch
Hotbox Heaters Ltd, Mill Lane, Lymington, Hants. Foil bench
heating and natural or bottled gas automatic heaters etc.
Natural Pest Control Ltd., Watermead, Yapton Road,
Barnham, Bognor Regis, W. Sussex PO22 6BQ
(Suppliers of predators)

Containers etc

Ceebrite Ltd, New Hertford House, St Albans Road, Watford,
Herts (bottles)
Walter Feltham & Son Ltd, 6 Caxton Road, London N22 6BT
(cloth bags)
GPG Containers, Luton Road, Dunstable, Beds LU5 4LN
Polybags Ltd, Atcraft Works, 197 Ealing Road, Wembley,
Middlesex

Labels and tickets

Able Label, Steepleprint Ltd, Earls Barton, Northampton NN6
0LS

Buralls of Wisbech, PO Box 7, Oldfield Lane, Wisbech,
Cambridge PE13 2SZ (plant labels)

Easiprints, Woodhouse Street, Leeds LS6 2YY

Improved Marking and Label Co Ltd, Nether Lane, Eccles-
field, Sheffield S30 3ZF (plant labels)

Kappy Products, Kappy House, Windlesham Road, West End,
Woking, Surrey

Minilabel, PO Box 134, Haywards Heath, West Sussex

William Sessions Ltd, The Ebor Press, Huntingdon Road,
York YO3 9HS

Promotional material including self-adhesive colour prints and leaflets

Just Leaflets, 10 Beulah Road, Wimbledon, London SW19 3SB

Miniprints, The Old Mill, Ribchester, Preston, Lancs PR3
2YN

Photoleaflets, Woodhouse Street, Leeds LS6 2PY

Polystyrene propagation trays and postal packs

Accelerated Propagation Ltd, Vines Cross, Heathfield, Sussex

Postal service and information

Post Office, Direct Mail Section, Room 195, 33 Grosvenor
Place, London SW1 1EE

Index